FIRST LIG

First Light

Paul Wharton

Brisance Books

With special thanks to Miles Bailey and his team at The Choir Press whose advice and professional touches turned what was an essay into a book.

First published in the United Kingdom in 2009 by
Brisance Books

ISBN 978-0-9563529-0-3 (hardback)
ISBN 978-0-9563529-1-0 (paperback)

Book production by The Choir Press, Gloucester

Contents

Dedication

This book is dedicated to the memory and also the families of those members of 321 EOD Company RAOC who were killed as a result of enemy action

Operators

Capt Stewardson	(29)	9th Sep 1971
WO2 Davies	(38)	4th Nov 1971
SSgt Cracknell	(29)	15th Mar 1972
Sgt Butcher	(24)	15th Mar 1972
Major Calladene	(39)	29th Mar 1972
Capt Young	(27)	15th Jul 1972
WO2 Clark	(34)	3rd Aug 1972
SSgt Hills	(28)	5th Dec 1972
Capt Gritten	(29)	21st Jun 1973
SSgt Beckett	(36)	30th Aug 1973
SSgt Brammah	(31)	18th Feb 1974
SSgt Rose	(30)	7th Nov 1974
WO2 Maddocks	(32)	2nd Dec 1974
WO2 Garside	(34)	17th Jul 1975
Sgt Walsh	(28)	9th Jan 1977
WO2 O'Neill	(34)	31st May 1981
WO2 Howard	(29)	8th Jul 1988

In support

Cpl Brown	(25)	17th Jul 1975
Sig Reece	(18)	2nd Aug 1979
Gnr Furminger	(19)	2nd Aug 1979

Abbreviations

ATO	Ammunition Technical Officer
CATO	Chief Ammunition Technical Officer
CO	Commanding Officer
COP	Close Observation Platoon
CSE	Combined Services Entertainment
ECM	Electronic Counter Measures
EOD	Explosive Ordnance Disposal
GOC	General Officer Commanding
HME	Home-made explosive
IED	Improvised Explosive Device
IEDD	Improvised Explosive Device Disposal
MID	Mentioned in Despatches
MoD	Ministry of Defence
NB	Nitrobenzene
NTH	Newtownhamilton
PIRA	Provisional Irish Republican Army
RAOC	Royal Army Ordnance Corps
RC	Radio controlled
RCV	Remote Control Vehicle
RE	Royal Engineer
RESA	Royal Engineer Search Adviser
REST	Royal Engineer Search Team
RGJ	Royal Green Jackets
RNAD	Royal Navy Armaments Depot
RPG	Rocket Propelled Grenade
RSP	Render Safe Procedure
RUC	Royal Ulster Constabulary
RV	Rendezvous
SAS	Special Air Service / Special Ammunition Stowage
SATO	Senior Ammunition Technical Officer
SF	Security Forces
TPU	Time and Power Unit
UDR	Ulster Defence Regiment
WIS	Weapons Intelligence Section, Royal Military Police
XMG	Crossmaglen

For my parents who guided me
For Jen who had to wait for me
For my children who fulfil me
For Ros who enriches me

Preface

One autumnal evening as I idly sifted through my Bomb Disposal reports, memorabilia and disintegrating photo album, the build-up to the 5th November annual battlefest was gathering pace outside the house. It doesn't happen too often and a whiff of gunpowder is quite different to the pungent stench of blasted high explosives, yet this time it was enough to bring my previous life back into focus. That evening amid the intermittent flash and thud of fireworks I sat and thought again of those cold boggy fields of South Armagh which had dragged at our vehicles as they skidded and strained to haul out, or just to move, the highly hazardous loads I had tethered to the end of a long rope. Where each gateway and every gap in the myriad of grey stone walls was potentially lethal. Where tinkling brooks disappeared into deadly culverts. Who of us with this experience could forget the adrenalin-high excitement of the current job? Without too much effort my nose might again wrinkle at the overpowering carcinogenic reek of a home-made explosive (HME) that smelled of marzipan and impregnated everything it touched. I imagined I could hear the ribald joking and laughter of the people I lived and worked with and conversely it would be so easy, even now, to weep for good people devastated by the conflict's cruel ironies. The 30-year Irish conflict was much more intense than many people on the mainland probably realise. A total of 3,350 British people were killed and a further 47,500 injured. In just one year, 1972, at the very apex of the violence, terrorists succeeded in killing 100 British soldiers and wounding 500 more. In 1972 six of those deaths were Bomb Disposal Operators.

The 30-year Irish conflict was much more intense than many people on the mainland probably realise. A total of 3,350 British people were killed and a further 47,500 injured. In just one year, 1972, at the very apex of the violence, terrorists succeeded in killing 100 British soldiers and wounding 500 more. In 1972 six of those deaths were Bomb Disposal Operators.

In deciding to publish my Bomb Disposal experiences, primarily those of my third tour of duty, my initial intention had been to provide my family with a narrative of what it was to have been a Bomb Disposal Operator during the Northern Ireland Campaign. Thrown into a box with the rest of my military memorabilia, the book might surface one day to put all the accompanying bits and bobs into some sort of context. Today I work for a large pharmaceutical wholesaler in a job where risk is also a key factor, but any failure is a cost borne by the bottom line. It doesn't have the same serious and devastating repercussions on my family. Yes, it's a different world from the one I and my colleagues inhabited all those years ago.

As the book took shape, I realised it was also an opportunity to highlight something that has vexed me for a very long time. Why is it that none of the 17 Royal Army Ordnance Corps Bomb Disposal Operators killed during the Northern Ireland Campaign were awarded a posthumous gallantry medal? Not one of them was *recognised* in this way. It appears to be a question that dare not speak its name. Why? This anomaly stands out even more starkly when compared to others killed in similar circumstances over a similar period. In London, a George Cross and George Medal were awarded to two members of the Metropolitan Police Bomb Squad killed attempting to neutralise IRA devices and in the Falklands Campaign a Navy Conspicuous Gallantry Medal was awarded to the Royal Engineer Bomb Disposal Operator who lost his life attempting to defuse an Argentinean aircraft bomb on board a ship. In fact almost every large war-time bomb defused by the Royal Engineers results in a formal recognition for their Operator. Yet if you were to ask most people to hazard a guess as to what is more dangerous to the man defusing it – a 500kg iron bomb with a military fuze or a 5kg explosive device with an improvised firing mechanism – I doubt that the iron bomb would come out on top as often as the improvised bomb. I'm not saying all

Why is it that none of the 17 Royal Army Ordnance Corps Bomb Disposal Operators killed during the Northern Ireland Campaign were awarded a posthumous gallantry medal?

unexploded iron bombs are safe, I'm simply pointing out what I see as an anomaly in how 'the system' recognised our efforts. Clearly the Royal Engineers have a different view of this work than our people. Futhermore, can it be that the number of TV cameras at a bomb incident is a measure of an Operator's gallantry. Discuss!

So this book will also say something about the men who died. Not about who they were, how, or even why most of them died. It's about the type of dangers they faced which proved fatal for them and a catastrophe for their families. These hazards were faced up to by all members of my profession who served in this capacity and I hope the book will also provide a testimony to many others whose contribution wasn't felt to be sufficiently worthy to be formally recognised by the system, yet who faced up to the same dangers.

I think there are questions to be asked of our hierarchy in the first place who set the bar high, of historians, our media, civil servants and even politicians who appear to value only the soldiers who receive medals yet too easily ignore the contribution of the rest. Clearly they have more faith in the medals system than I have. The talk is often of 'winning' medals: ie there will be winners and losers. Well if so it smacks more of the lottery to me than a credible system for recognising and rewarding those who put their life on the line for others.

I hope my own experiences will paint a context for the work, what it entailed and the unstable, volatile nature of it all. You might conclude, with me, just how easy it was to die if your luck abandoned you.

Some may think that the more time a person spends at this work and the more experienced he becomes, the better at it he becomes; that any near misses he experiences might add value to that experience and it is by applying the rules that he has the best chance of making it through. But I would maintain that none of that is relevant if your luck eventually runs out on you. For everything you have learnt or experienced before will not protect you if at that crucial time, just once, you underestimate, interpret incorrectly or misunderstand what is in front of you. The more time you spend at this work, the more the odds increase that this is what is going to happen. I had my share of misinterpretations and came close to disaster on more than one occasion, so I can say with hand on heart, there but for the grace of God . . .

Bomb Disposal Operators in the Northern Ireland conflict only had to serve two tours of duty as an Operator. It was enough.

1st Tour – 1974

I first got a taste for the tricks of this trade when I attended a short introductory course on bomb disposal in 1970. I was 19 years old and the course was one of a number of different modules that came at the end of a three-year Ammunition Technician Class 2 apprenticeship at the Army Apprentice College near Chepstow. That one-week bomb disposal course was followed a couple of years later by another two-week bomb disposal module which formed part of a larger course that would see me upgraded from an Ammunition Technician Class 2 to 1. Throughout this period Operator losses in Northern Ireland were a regular and almost routine event. There was, in my mind anyway, a sense of unreality about it all. I say this mainly because the guys were all much senior to me and I didn't know any of them. Then on 3rd August 1972 all the talk at my unit was around Warrant Officer Class 2 'Nobby' Clark; a family man from our unit whom I did know personally. He'd been killed near Clady whilst trying to clear a device in a milk churn. I think I can say that at that point the dangers associated with this work finally struck home.

I attended an NI Pre-Operations course in early 1974 and I caught the Liverpool to Belfast ferry in April of that year. I was to be the No. 2, the Operator's Assistant, on a team that operated out of Lisanelly Barracks in Omagh. From there we would support the resident battalion, the 1st Royal Tank Regiment.

Our tactical area of responsibility encompassed much of counties Tyrone and Fermanagh. This is a large area with a porous international border and the tour was quite eventful. The team was headed up by Staff Sergeant Lou Bean. Lou was known by the units he supported as the ATO, since in Northern Ireland all Operators were collectively called Ammunition Technical Officers, or ATOs for short. ATOs could be any rank from Sergeant through to Captain. I hope Lou will not mind me saying that he is a prime example of someone who despite neutralising a number of large devices and being a credit to the Corps didn't receive recognition for it. This may not have bothered him too much, but later it began to bother me.

Pre-Operations Course. In the back row, far right, is Staff Sergeant Lou Bean (No. 16). I'm in the middle at the front in the combat kit (No. 10). Second from the left in the front row is Sergeant Mick O'Neill (No. 4). I'll speak about Mick later in the book.

Green vehicle movements were allowed throughout Tyrone and Fermanagh and we traversed the counties daily in support of Security Forces (SF) operations. I wasn't too happy at being issued with a mere 9mm pistol since they are effective only up to about 30 metres. I therefore carried one of the team's 12-bore semi-automatic shotguns loaded with a mixture of shot. Fortunately I never had to use it against a person or I would have been in trouble since I'm sure it wasn't approved for use in that way and I would almost certainly have infringed the rights of anyone trying to kill me.

The only high-velocity shots I heard fired in anger during that tour were from me – and then it was at a car. On this occasion we were called to clear a vehicle which had been abandoned on the border. When we arrived the air was thick with mosquitoes. Some of the troops who had been on the ground for some time could hardly see, their faces were so swollen. Lou wanted the car cleared quickly. I said I could help to do this if I could be provided with a rifle, which I duly was. In those days I was a bit of a marksman. I put two shots into the fuel tank and then reloaded the rifle with a tracer round which I put into the growing pool of leaking fuel. The car burned out and so we could be sure there was nothing sinister contained inside it. We were out of there in double quick time and so were the ground troops. Any innovation that helps get the thing completed from a distance is what's called for and you

Green vehicles

In northern Ireland the army refer to their standard military vehicles as 'green', as opposed to covert military vehicles which might be any type or colour to blend in with the populace and their surroundings. The latter could more easily go where 'green' vehicles were too much of a target.

make the best use of anything you can get your hands on. That's a fairly well-established philosophy.

We got around the 'estate' in a Safari five-door Land-Rover which had a horse box attached that was designed to take our Remote Control Vehicle Wheelbarrow. If we had to turn the Land-Rover around quickly in a narrow lane it was a logistical, time-consuming nightmare. This vehicle configuration would soon be superseded by lightly armoured Ford Transits. In fact all the equipment and technology available to us was changing apace throughout this period. New versions of Wheelbarrow would come on stream every few months, as would new explosive tools, and especially welcome were improvements in the equipment for tackling radio controlled devices. There was no shortage of investment by the MoD in those days. To provide a flavour of the tour, I've summarised it with photos taken at some of the incidents we covered.

Getting around by vehicle was time consuming and occasionally we resorted to helicopters. I have to say that, from the air, the undulating countryside of both these rural counties was a picture book of little villages, green fields and silver lakes ...

Main street Castelderg. As we arrived on the scene a small device exploded in the car. The ATO is taking a quick look.

In case there is a secondary device the ATO has set the car on fire since a burnt-out car is a car cleared. We await events as I reel in the electrical firing cable.

Two SF Land–Rovers were ambushed making their way back from supporting us in an investigation of a bus explosion. A Command Wire device detonated under the second Land-Rover caused it to somersault up the road. The only reason our team didn't use this road is that we attended the incident by helicopter.

The escort in the front passenger seat wasn't thrown clear and he was crushed by the vehicle. This was the first body I had ever seen and I was somewhat transfixed by the tragedy. The ATO had to snap me out of my contemplation. I was always shocked by similar sights because they brought home just how mortal we all are and how we are potentially just one journey from disaster.

The upper floor of the Deanery at Clogher was used as an operational headquarters for a UDR unit. One evening it came under attack from two groups of gunmen. Mortars and two RPG-7 rockets were fired in the attack. The skeleton staff at the HQ were almost overwhelmed but the day was saved by the coincidental arrival of two Scout cars from the Royal Tank Regiment. During the attack Woman Private Eva Martin was struck in the head as she passed by a staircase window and killed. She was the first woman soldier to die in the Campaign.

Eva Martin.

PIRA mortar bombs abandoned during the attack. The ATO has asked me to remove their propelling charges prior to destroying them in a controlled explosion.

An explosion was reported at this barn. We found blood and a part collapsed roof so an 'own goal' was suspected. However we also detected a radio control signal.

After jamming any radio control firing signal the ATO went forward and discovered a milk churn under the collapsed roof.

He then discovered another milk churn and subsequently two more. These were all linked by detonating cord.

Finally in the roof he discovered the radio control firing switch and the detonator. The incident had been an elaborate 'come on' to try and entice SF into a killing zone.

After intercepting two armed men in a car SF decided to investigate this remote farm.

SF found this large car bomb in situ, which was apparently on its way to Enniskillen.

[above] We destroyed five sacks of explosives in a series of controlled explosions.

[left] In fact the whole place was a Quartermaster's store of arms and bomb-making equipment.

This crater was produced by just one sack of the home-made explosives.

Under this small bridge SF discovered a large device in milk churns which would have been detonated by Command Wire.

One milk churn has been extracted: more to follow.

Destroying the device in a series of controlled explosions.

The out station at Rosslea was attacked one night by proxy. The driver who'd been hijacked and had a bomb loaded onto his van left it outside the security wall but didn't tell anyone. Fortunately despite the extensive damage there were no casualties. Interestingly there was absolutely nothing left that was discernable of the van.

We didn't have far to travel to this one – about 200 metres from Lisanelly camp. We worked on the van bomb for about 30 minutes from the other side of the building, but our equipment became tangled at the sharp end in our firing cables. Eventually we fired the 'flying plate' Beguine even though it had spun around and was facing the wrong way (see 'From the passive to the offensive'). The vehicle caught fire but 15 minutes later the device functioned. You end up struggling with your mate to get in or under the vehicle because you know that everything that went up is going to come down.

The Crown building was wrecked. 5,000 chickens held in an adjacent farm were decimated and our Remote Control Vehicle Wheelbarrow was written off.

Towards the end of my four-month tour at the Omagh Section, I was transferred to the headquarters at Lisburn, primarily to assist the Warrant Officer ATO who was seconded to the Forensic Science Laboratory. An incident occurred at Lisburn which is worth mentioning because I think it helps to illustrate that actually, Operators, despite the Hollywood hype, are really nothing more nor less than a cross-section of the populace with all the idiosyncrasies and personality weaknesses that people get by with. I call this incident the 'Isandlwana moment' and it went like this. 'Foxtrot' was the reserve team based at Lisburn and it hadn't been deployed for quite some time. The team's vehicle had therefore been de-kitted of all its equipment. Our HQ would be closed at night and in order that the duty Operator could access the equipment during silent hours it was kept in the cellar at the HQ Lisburn guardroom. On this occasion it was about midday and a 'disruption day' was on the go in Belfast. A number of car bombs were being dealt with and all the Belfast teams had been committed. The Foxtrot team, in the military vernacular, was to be 'stood to' so that it could respond immediately to an operational tasking order when it came. I was told to get myself over to the guardroom asap to help a certain ATO Captain get Foxtrot up and running. I approached the guardroom at the gallop and as I did so the wind in my ears didn't prevent me from hearing a strange sound emanating from the guardroom: a sort of strangled cry like someone in pain, or perhaps even a wounded animal.

'What the hell is that?' I wondered, as you do.

Bursting into the guardroom I scanned the room and it was easy to see from the worried faces of the soldiers standing around that all was not well. And sure enough there came another strangled cry followed by some crashing and thumping from the cellar.

'Where's the ATO?' I asked somewhat unnecessarily, for already a possible scenario was beginning to dawn on me.

Someone pointed to the stairs and apprehensively I descended. I was greeted, as they say, by an amazing sight. The ATO, red in face and breathing heavily, had completely lost it. The reason was sitting defiantly between us on the floor of the cellar. The Quartermaster, for accounting and security purposes, had had the Foxtrot team equipment neatly packed into a wooden crate and this had been securely bound with metal banding tape. If cutting equipment had originally been left there ... well, there was no evidence of it now.

The ATO's despair, frustration and anger at the situation had got the better of him and he was now looking for someone to kill. At the moment he was taking it out on the crate.

As I watched from the safety of the staircase, the officer gave a further strangled cry and cursing and swearing he launched himself once more at the crate, booting it with both feet in turn but alas in vain. It was, with hindsight, pure comedy of the Fawlty Towers ilk. Gasping to catch his breath for a moment he paused and I saw my opportunity. I leapt across the room to place myself between him and the abused box. I asked him to calm down. The reputation of the cool, calm and collected ATO was now in tatters, at least at the Lisburn HQ guardroom. He responded to the suggestion and so I didn't have to hit him.

Someone shot off to the Stores to get some cutting equipment and eventually with the Improvised Explosive Device Disposal (IEDD) kit loaded onto his vehicle we sent him off to the war. I'll give him his due, he did thank me afterwards for my help in getting him through what he thought was a short period of stress.

But he was highly strung at any time and had a reputation for smashing telephone receivers. But this, shall we say, personality quirk, hadn't prevented him from becoming an Operator. The psychometric testing we all had to undergo wasn't a very useful tool if it was supposed to filter out at source the temperamental. In fact I'm sceptical as to whether it really filtered out anyone who was really unsuitable since a veritable cross-section of characters always remained within the profession.

I have likened the Lisburn guardroom incident to the disaster at Isandlwana in South Africa in 1879. Here it was with a Zulu army bearing down on them that the British troops found out, too late, that for accounting and security purposes the Quartermaster had centralised the rifle ammunition and it was held in inaccessible packaging. You know this because you've seen the film *Zulu Dawn*. On that earlier occasion the troops were going to be put to the assegai, so I have every sympathy with anyone then if they had blown a fuze and strangled the Quartermaster.

2nd Tour – 1975–76

The following year in June, newly promoted to Sergeant and married only a fortnight, I was posted back to Lisburn and onto the permanent staff at the unit's headquarters. This time it was for a 12-month stint mainly to handle the unit's reports and to collate statistical data. It was an accompanied posting and I was provided with a married quarter. Living there with my wife was quite civilised but at times it was quite surreal. People could get very energised about stock checks and audits etc. So on the one hand it felt like a peacetime posting and when normality reigned it seemed ... well, normal. On the other hand I could spend a day sweating it out down town which on any given day might have more in common with Beirut in the bad old days than Great Britain, but when I returned to the Mess the topic was still about stock checks and bloody audits.

Within a week of taking up the post the team from Bessbrook dropped in at the headquarters to pick up some equipment. We briefly touched on old times since Gus Garside, the Operator, had been one of my instructors at the Apprentice College and his No. 2, Cal Brown, was a friend and colleague from the unit in the UK I had just left. I remember that moment well all these years on. But within a week the team had been wiped out. They were both killed with two other soldiers as they deployed from a helicopter at Cortreasla Bridge, Forkhill to deal with some suspicious objects. A device comprising 50–100lb of home-made explosives (HME) was detonated alongside them as they negotiated the edge of a field. The Command Wire-type device was initiated by a local unemployed coach builder who, on seeing the opportunity, had scrambled to a vantage point across the other side of the field. He was in fact arrested that afternoon. As a result of this tragedy our Render Safe Procedures (RSPs) in the rural areas were amended.

The team's belongings were repatriated via the HQ at Lisburn. Their damaged weapons and burnt flack jackets were a sad and sorry sight.

The unit headquarters had an operational area of responsibility which covered Counties Antrim and some of Down and also provided a backup to the Belfast Section. As a member of the HQ 'back office' staff an Operator wasn't immune to the omnipresent dangers. On one particular February morning in '76 my day started calmly enough but this changed when I was unexpectedly caught up in a big, fast-moving incident. By the end of the day it had almost ended in disaster.

Called in to support the Belfast Section, my team and I were tasked to provide cover for the city centre. Accordingly we were deployed to the Grand Central Hotel on Royal Avenue – or GCH as it was called – to await events. This old Victorian hotel was at the end of its natural life and was being used as a barracks for a few hundred soldiers. It was often a target for car bombs, but not so often that I might have anticipated it happening today. So sure enough PIRA (the Provisional IRA) attacked it via the adjacent GPO Sorting Office building. I would find out later that the Sorting Office was separated from the GCH only by a narrow street that ran parallel to Royal Avenue. This narrow street was within the GCH security complex and the military used it as a vehicle park.

The first I knew that we were under attack was when the bomb alarm went off with a deafening wail and the well-practised evacuation drill kicked in for real. The place immediately burst into life with soldiers pouring out of every room and spilling down the main staircase into Royal Avenue. If I was to know what was going on I would have to get to the Ops room on an upper floor, but this wasn't easy. My work was cut out just trying to get up the stairs since there was a veritable wall of soldiers travelling equally forcibly in the opposite direction. Eventually arriving at the Ops room, I found the staff there were more concerned with evacuating the room than briefing me. All I got from a Captain as he pushed past me with a pile of files in his arms was, 'There's a bomb in the GPO Sorting Office.' And before I could say, 'Where the hell is the Sorting Office?' – he was gone! I didn't remember a scenario anything like this on the Pre-Ops course exercises. There you'd ask a pertinent question and by jingo you received a pertinent answer – which is a good basis for decision making . . .

To be on scene at this very early juncture is unusual for an Operator and I was now caught up in the confusion and chaos that accompanied the evacuation of the buildings. With no tangible information to go on my mind was racing trying to work out what to do next. Outside in Royal Avenue I soon realised that accessing the team equipment was going to be problematic once I discovered that our vehicle was inconveniently parked up against the Sorting Office building wall. As I tentatively peered around the street corner contemplating whether we should risk a sortie into the danger area to recover it, a smallish device exploded in the Sorting Office with a loud bang that echoed up and down the narrow street, blowing out some windows on the first floor. I then saw that the building hadn't been fully evacuated of civilians. Forward of the security cordon, now without a radio, I was on the spot. Metaphorically speaking, I took off my ATO hat and behaved as I think any member of the Security Forces might well have done: I carried out a quick foray into the building to make sure no one else remained, calling out as I went. There wasn't, and for my trouble, as I was leaving a mezzanine floor a second small device detonated above a doorway just a second or two after I had walked through it. Either I stumbled or the blast blew me down the staircase. I landed upside down in a heap at the bottom of the stairwell, covered in plaster. I was unharmed but I had the strange sensation that the hairs on the back of my neck were quite erect. I picked myself up and stumbled to the building entrance. I was somewhat surprised therefore to find I had been locked in behind 15-foot metal gates. The Boilerman, whose very presence had caused me to enter the building, had left the scene but only after securing the gates behind him. I only managed to escape the building after my No. 2, Lance Corporal Coates, discovering my predicament, went off and dragged the Boilerman back to the gate.

Someone had prematurely shouted, 'The ATO's copped it!' and before I could even catch my breath, the security cordon around GCH collapsed. To my dismay I was faced with a whole bevy of soldiers heading towards me down the narrow street. With two small devices having functioned and the high likelihood that a much bigger one was not far behind them, a lot of people were about to be killed. I was suddenly gripped by fear. In my urgency to get everyone out of the danger area I'm afraid I was none too polite in requesting the soldiers leave the scene. Let me state now, a little late, my apologies to the Commanding Officer of the Regiment whom I didn't recognise till afterwards and who got the worst of my tongue!

A few minutes later we were all safe at the front of GCH in Royal Avenue and the cordon was re-established. Breathing heavily and with my hands shaking like leaves in a storm I realised all of a sudden that I was surrounded by people. Royal Avenue was teeming with both civilians and soldiers. People were asking me lots of questions and I wasn't giving many answers. I was a bit shocked I guess. I was trying to pull myself together when all of a sudden a substantial '*baboom*' thundered out from the other side of the GCH building. It was a massive blast that sounded something like the van bomb at the Crown

Buildings Omagh all those years ago. The effect was to blow away all the hubbub around me and for a split second there was silence. The silence was followed almost immediately by the familiar tinkling sound of glass falling like heavy rain into the streets behind me.

I would discover later that I had unknowingly walked past the van bomb when I was checking out the place.

Aftermath. The narrow street which separated the Grand Central Hotel on the left from the GPO Sorting Office on the right. Military vehicles damaged by the blast remain in situ.

PW in discussion with the Royal Engineer Searchers post final clearance

The spot up against the wall where our team vehicle had been parked. Inside the building the large diesel tank that the fire brigade had been so worried about can just be seen.

As I walked around this scene of devastation next day I contemplated just how tenuous life can be as an ATO and it's not only your life that's on the line: your entire career can be up there too, for mistakes are not easily forgiven.

The damage was quite extensive to all rooms on that side of the GCH building, not to mention the Sorting Office. A breeze block guardroom built on to the GCH as a blister was completely wrecked. Some military Land-Rovers were written off and security sensitive papers which had been sucked out of various shattered windows were now blowing around the street, much to the annoyance of their owners running around trying to collect them all up. My armoured vehicle was barely driveable since it had sustained a damaged wheel and was stripped of its blue light and aerials and covered in rubble.

Control was tightened up and no one was to be allowed into the danger area. I was approached then by the Fire Brigade who wanted to enter the area to extinguish a fire that was threatening a 5,000-gallon tank of diesel in the Sorting Office used for refuelling GPO vehicles. They insisted and so I took the opportunity, with my No. 2, to go forward with them and reconnoitre the damage. We pulled all the rubble off our vehicle and then Lance Corporal Coates recovered it. I watched as it limped away into safety with its seriously wobbly wheel. We all withdrew behind the cordon then and 30 minutes later a further, small device detonated in the same building. With daylight fading fast the Sorting Office was secured overnight and no one was allowed in.

Overall, a disaster had been averted simply by good luck more than anyone's good judgement.

The building was searched next day and found to be clear of any further devices, albeit I destroyed in a controlled explosion a duffle bag containing someone's lunch which the owner had abandoned.

This incident demonstrates to me how dangers unexpectedly and quickly strike from left field when you live and work within this genre. You try to apply the training principles but fast-moving events can get the better of you. If they do and you have done something wrong, then you're in trouble. We are our own worst critics. I'm pretty certain that if I or anyone else had been killed or injured in the incident, then I, as the Operator at the scene, would probably have received a good deal of flack over it. The chaos and confusion which reigned at the time would have been history by the time my role and immediate actions were analysed in the light of our strict operating procedures. The profession

I'm pretty certain that if I or anyone else had been killed or injured in the incident, then I, as the Operator at the scene, would probably have received a good deal of flack over it. The chaos and confusion which reigned at the time would have been history by the time my role and immediate actions were analysed in the light of our strict operating procedures.

was bound up by this type of thinking at that time and I'll comment further on this matter later in the book. As it happened the incident was passed off as pretty much a routine matter. Lt Colonel Underhill was interviewed that evening in the street by Trevor McDonald for the BBC News to explain to the Ulster people why their mail was going to be delivered a little later than usual.

In the immediate aftermath of the vehicle bomb explosion a policeman brought a postman over to me and I was able to ask him a few questions. It was he who had driven the large vehicle bomb into the Sorting Office. At the time I thought he'd been coerced into it but later he would admit to some complicity. I guess he could have said he'd been put under duress since proxy type incidents were very common at this time. I was sitting in the Crumlin Road Crown Court later that year when the sentence was passed. Well, to be honest I felt only sadness for him and his family. Living in Andersons Town, a mainly Republican area, he had been made an offer he couldn't refuse and in the end he was probably the only real victim of the incident. He was the same age as me. Despite protestations that he had never been a member of PIRA and the efforts of his 'brief' to mitigate his role in the attack, he was sent down for 15 years.

Proxy bombs

PIRA would often hijack a vehicle with two occupants. A bomb would be loaded on board. Holding one of the occupants hostage, the other would be ordered to drive the vehicle and bomb to the target. If the vehicle was stopped on the way to the target the Security Forces had to remember they were dealing with innocent parties. The attacks were often less than successful since the vehicle would often be abandoned by its frightened owner without being placed in the optimum spot. Nonetheless this modus operandi significantly reduced the risk to PIRA members.

During this tour I had my fair share of incendiary devices to deal with. These devices were mainly of Protestant origin. They were often crude and targeted against Catholics living in the Larne area. On one occasion because the room was inaccessible to my remote control equipment I had to enter it myself. The floor was covered in diesel fuel and right in the middle of it two small incendiary devices in cigarette packets had been placed with the intention of igniting the fuel. I'm not sure how much the suit would have protected me if the whole thing had gone up. Having your No. 2 standing by with a fire extinguisher was always a good idea in these circumstances.

On another occasion two incendiary devices placed on a bus were subsequently confirmed by the Forensic Science Laboratory as having chemical components that did not in fact react with each other – and so the devices were effectively inert. This knowledge subsequently led me to adopt a Render Safe Procedure that with hindsight I wished I'd tackled differently. One evening I was tasked to deal with an attack that had occurred on a Catholic school in Larne. Prior to my arrival someone had gallantly, or foolishly depending on your point of view, placed the device into a sand-filled bucket which had been left on top of a desk. The device itself comprised about 5kg of an incendiary mix contained inside a large glass chemical bottle. The 'switch' was of a chemical delay type, like the devices on the bus previously. This chemical initiator was half stuffed into the neck of the bottle. The bottle was unfortunately well protected from my disruptive equipment by the sides of the metal bucket. What to do?

I surmised that because the previous incendiary devices had been inert this might well be the same. I therefore decided to risk lifting out the chemical initiator. Briefing my No. 2, Corporal Spencer, I asked him to wait outside of the room with a fire extinguisher at the ready. Taking a deep breath I leant over the desk and took a firm hold of the initiator. It was tight and at first it wouldn't budge. I pulled a little harder and then '*pssst*' – it was the telltale sound of acid dropping onto the incendiary mix. The device initiated and I just had time to throw myself backwards across the room. Increasing in intensity and with a roar the device went up like a regular Vesuvius. As the bottle melted before my very eyes the white hot flames soared, up peeling the paint from the high classroom ceiling. This inferno lasted for about 5–10 seconds. Right on cue Corporal Spencer appeared in the doorway with the fire extinguisher in hand and a look on his face as if he was expecting to have to turn it on me. His arrival was about the only thing that went right with the plan, for the CO_2 extinguisher was useless against the oxygenated inferno. Nonetheless it would have prevented the flames from spreading had they not been confined to the sand-filled bucket. As jet black smoke filled up the room, I was grateful the thing hadn't exploded. Little collateral damage, but I have to say, not my finest moment.

Throughout my time with the headquarters the Ops phone on my desk would ring and with just a short explanation of the task, the location and the contact at the scene, the duty team would crash out. Often the calls would occur in the middle of the night and when I was the duty Operator the team would collect me from my married quarter. On one occasion my mother came to stay with us. Woken up by both the blue flashing lights and the animated radio traffic, it was a bit disconcerting for her to see her only son disappear on a mission to God knows where, fearing I was never going to come back. With the benefit of hindsight I recommend Operators don't let their mothers get that close to the action! Again it was this Lisburn anomally of being a peacetime unit but very much part of a war.

My 12 months with the Headquarters was interesting, exciting and often eventful. Notwithstanding the misery the people of Northern Ireland were being put through, I have to say I thoroughly enjoyed my time there.

A weekend of disruption by Protestant militants had all teams in and around Belfast flat out dealing with hundreds of hoax devices. A complete distraction. The picture shows four I was tasked to. Hoax devices could be quite sophisticated. The cylinder on the left even has a mercury tilt switch wired in. All the time I was dealing with these devices the radio traffic was red hot with the SF on the ground at Randlestown pleading for ATO assistance for a car bomb. Eventually the car bomb went off before anyone was tasked to it.

This is a Protestant UVF terrorist cache of bomb-making materials. I spent a lot of time chasing them around Antrim dealing with their devices – at least five were probably down to them. I got the impression over time that the Protestant terrorist organisations were even more ruthless in their targetting than PIRA.

I would come across exactly this type of device again and was able to neutralise one that had been placed, mistakenly I guess, on a Protestant family's window ledge.'

I gave evidence at the court case that sent down the UVF boys whose explosive cache it was and who wore these masks. At the trial the defence lawyer fiercely grilled a police officer who had been shot by one of them, such that I offered my sympathy to him when we met up later. He told me that at one point he had begun to wonder whether he had in fact been shot at all.

Shortly after commencing my tour at the Headquarters in Lisburn, the Bessbrook ATO, his No. 2, a Royal Engineer Search Adviser and a Major from the Green Howards were all killed in an explosion whilst deploying to a task from a helicopter. This is one of the aerial photographs that was used to plan the operation. As the soldiers negotiated a stile, a device buried alongside the signpost was detonated by a Command Wire. The guy who murdered them was arrested that afternoon.The ATO had been an instructor at the Army College during my apprenticeship there and the No. 2 and I had served together very recently.

The driver of this proxy-type device had been ordered to take a bomb into Aldergrove airport. Bravely he drove the vehicle through the airport complex to some waste ground where the device eventually exploded harmlessly.

This is Bow Street in Lisburn where my wife and I would often go shopping. I had just received the tasking message from HQ 39 Brigade when the room shook as the vehicle-borne device detonated.

Workmen reported an explosion in close proximity to their hut at a building site in Lisburn. At first there was no obvious evidence of this and I have Wheelbarrow carrying out a Recce.

At some point you have to make an approach. Here I am searching around and under the hut, and there it was jammed in between the hut and the adjacent wall. Not easy to get at.

The device in a Tupperware container had partially exploded in that the detonator had functioned but this had not propagated to the main charge. The type of explosives would suggest that the device was of a Protestand terrorist origin.

Within a week of completing my tour I was called to Antrim to deal with a truck load of mortars pointing into the Royal Navy Armaments Depot and adjacent army camp. The army had had the foresight to block the flight path of the mortars with the shovel of an armoured digger.

After firing two rounds of 84mm Carl Gustav at the truck to disrupt the electrical firing leads I blew the tyres on one side of the truck with a series of small explosive charges.

The sapper driver of the armoured digger gallantly agreed to tip the truck over.

We recovered 18 home-made mortar bombs and their tubes. Note the dent in one tube caused by the impact of a Carl Gustav projectile. The attack failed primarily because the mortar switching arrangement had self-destructed before it could fire the actual mortars. Within a short time this type of mortar bomb would be obsolete and PIRA would replace it with a bomb that had 30 times the payload and was a lot less complicated. For my contribution the RNAD presented me with a brass replica of a Londonderry cannon called Old Meg. I still have it.

One of the buggerance factors of serving in NI as an Operator was the subsequent court cases we were called to attend as expert witnesses. These attendances were highly onerous for some people who were called back from all parts of the world time and time again. People were brought back from Hong Kong for example only to have the case deferred for weeks or cancelled. Often the date for a hearing would be moved even as the ATO was in transit to it. Sometimes if your case was deferred or cancelled, the first you'd hear of it was in the Crumlin Road Court House café after standing around for two days waiting to be called. This café was a melting pot of defendants, their families and also their accusers. It was bizarre. For a start no one in authority seemed to have any concerns over the costs of this little lot or the time that was being wasted. If behind the scenes it was all spiffingly efficient, well it certainly didn't feel like that to us. On one particular occasion though I did feel that my attendance at court had been especially useful.

In the dock was a Protestant terrorist gang who had caused mayhem in the Larne area over a period of years. I think we'd met before in the abstract sense. These boys were trying to muddy the waters at their trial by claiming the SAS (Special Air Service) had been involved in the murder of a leading Catholic which they were being accused of. They said the Special Air Service had put them up to it. Evidence for the defence involved a British army ammunition container that the gang insisted had been given to them by the SAS.

Almost as a throwaway comment the prosecution barrister asked me if I knew anything about ammunition boxes, to which I replied, 'I do.' Taking me into a room he showed me the box in question. It was grey in colour and had 'SAS' stencilled on it in white paint. He asked me if Special Air Service ammunition containers would normally have the regiment's name written on them.

Later that day I was called to the witness box to give evidence in the same case in respect of a blast bomb I had neutralised. I was asked to explain how I had gone about it and the damage it would have done had it functioned. After I had given my evidence, the barrister suggested to the judge that I may be able to clarify matters in respect of the ammunition box and this was duly passed across for me to interpret the markings on it. It gave me great pleasure to be able to say that the box was a standard military package with standard markings. Grey paint signified the box would have contained chemical ammunition of the lachrymatory type, ie CS gas. Because the ammunition would produce irritant smoke, when transported by sea it must always be stored on deck. SAS therefore signified that the ammunition container required Special Ammunition Stowage. The waters were less muddy at the trial after that.

I was tasked to a total of seventy plus incidents during this tour of which 14 were categorised as live devices; mainly blast bombs and incendiaries.

3rd Tour – 1981

The high octane of the GPO Sorting Office and Antrim mortar incidents had receded into mere memory when five years later I was earmarked once again for another tour of duty. What goes around comes around as they say. This time it was to lead the section based in the little village of Bessbrook. I would provide cover for all the explosive-related incidents and support SF operations across the 'bandit country' of South Armagh. South Armagh by this time had gained a reputation all of its own.

In the intervening period I had been promoted twice more, had served in three different posts and the war in Ireland had become something of a backdrop to the day job, though the war was often on the agenda at regimental dinner nights whenever the 'lamps got swung' – which was probably too often as I'm sure our long-suffering and bored wives would attest.

1981 may not have been on the same scale as the early '70s but it was still a time of high activity on both the political and military fronts. A series of high-profile hunger strikes began in 1981 which resulted in the deaths of ten Republican prisoners. Not winning any concessions from the British Government for that strategy, a new realism was spawned and the green shoots of a political solution began to be seen from thereon in. 1981 was also the last big year for PIRA bombings and shootings. After this the statistics show that this type of violence tailed off, gradually, year by year.

My team and I did what we could to thwart PIRA's operational aspirations in that green and deadly land. Given a fair crack, we helped unravel and spoil their set pieces and made them safe or at the very least we cleared away their highly hazardous scrap. In this, my third and final tour of duty in Ulster, I served alongside soldiers of the 1st Battalion the Queens Lancashire Regiment and then the 1st Battalion the Royal Green Jackets; two fine infantry regiments. There were also the men and women of the Ulster Defence Regiment (UDR) and Royal Ulster Constabulary (RUC) whom I found to be extremely decent, cheerful people doing their best in a nightmare situation, caught as they were between religious rocks and hard politics. We were supported by the Royal Engineer Specialist Search Teams (REST) and RMP Weapons Intelligence Section (WIS) whose expertise I relied upon to keep me alive. The camaraderie everyone felt for each other, well at times you could almost touch it. This was the antithesis of what we felt for our secret, ruthless and technically advanced enemy who were so bound up trying to kill us. Such is the nature of war, because for all of us who served in Northern Ireland, and especially those who served in South Armagh, that's exactly what it felt like.

18th January 1981

The lie of the land

Politically, Ulster has always been a fractious place and for 12 years or so it has been at war with itself. This time around the bullet is accompanied by the bomb; the Improvised Explosive Device (IED). Prolific use of explosives is intended to bring the Province to its knees. It won't happen because for any government there is too much at stake, but you can't tell PIRA that. I'm 29 years old and a Warrant Officer Class 2, Ammunition Technician. It's the Ammunition Technicians of the Royal Army Ordnance Corps who are periodically plucked from the day job of inspecting, repairing and disposing of the army's large ammunition stocks to carry out a four-month tour in Northern Ireland tackling Terrorist IEDs. IED Disposal or IEDD is the official term for this type of bomb disposal. Prior to Northern Ireland our people walked up to IEDs in Borneo, Aden, Cyprus and also Hong Kong. This Campaign however is on a different scale to all those that went before. We have had to 'up' our game!

As I walk through Aldergrove airport into the arrivals area, I scan the people at the Military Movements desk. One young guy holds a card on which is written '321'. This catches my eye because 321 Explosive Ordnance Disposal (EOD) Company is the army unit which has been formed specifically to carry out and coordinate Bomb Disposal Operations in Ulster. I head for him and introduce myself. 'WO2 Wharton – are you waiting for me?' He is, we shake hands and he introduces himself as a Lance Corporal from the headquarters at Lisburn. I follow him to the airport café where two guys sit. One is a military escort, the other I recognise as a Staff Sergeant Ammunition Technician with whom I've served before. He's flown in from 3 Base Ammunition Depot in Germany and he's heading for the Belfast Section. I tell him I'm headed for the ATO Section at Bessbrook near Newry but he already knows. He and I have different types of battle to fight. His is shift work; fast and furious; quick responses that befit the protection of a city. The modus operandi for me is different; occasionally fast and furious but mainly slow and unhurried since in the countryside terrorists have plenty of time and space to set up attacks. Only second tour Operators serve there now. In South Armagh it is the unpicking of each puzzle that is the challenge for often what you see and hear is what they want you to see and hear. It may only be a few miles square but PIRA always has something on the go there. In South Armagh a 'gung ho' attitude to the work can and will quickly become a liability for everyone concerned.

In South Armagh it is the unpicking of each puzzle that is the challenge for often what you see and hear is what they want you to see and hear.

The drive out of the airport is convoluted, through various checkpoints and security points. For me though, the first hint that normality really doesn't live here is that I see British Police Officers in flack jackets carrying both automatic rifles and pistols as a matter of routine. I accept that this type of policing is pretty much an anathema to the desires of the British people and each time I come here I do find it oddly disturbing. But what's the alternative when invisible men are bent on killing you ? For my money these coppers, and the members of the local Ulster Defence Regiment, all of whom live on the civilian net, have to be the most courageous of all the SF.

Whilst there's nothing visible about us to say we're army, it's probably obvious to anyone who might be clocking us. Our driver doesn't hang about even though the area we're travelling through is considered safe, ie it is predominantly Unionist. Having said that, the Province is only 60 miles by 80; about the size of Yorkshire and Humberside together. Nowhere is really outside the reach of this enemy which is integrated into the populace and doesn't wear a uniform. Whilst there are many terrorist splinter groups operating across the Province, by far the most ambitious in their operations and the most technically competent are the Provisional IRA. We've come a long way in our knowledge of Improvised Explosive Devices and how they can be deployed – because so have they.

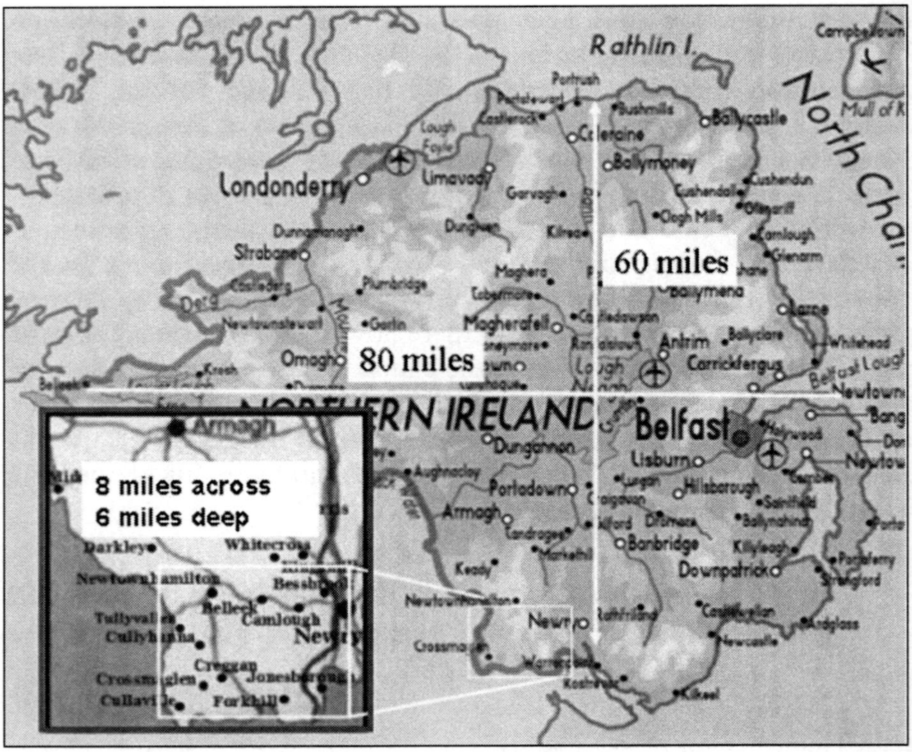

The bandit country of South Armagh. Small area, big trouble.

As the landscape flashes past I think of those who have gone before me. It's 10 years since the first IEDD Operator was killed and in the intervening period an additional 15 have died. I knew a number of them. They are our fallen, never to grow old, frozen forever into the space and time of our last meeting.

The drive to the British Army HQ at Lisburn takes about 20 minutes. HQ 321 EOD Company is one Portakabin complex among many. To date the unit has investigated over 12,000 incidents involving explosives. Half were live devices and neutralised. Most people will think the statistics quite an achievement.

I meet the unit Chief Clerk. I fill in a form with questions like – Have you made a will? – Next of kin? My photograph is taken and it is this that will appear in the newspapers if I don't make it through. Eventually I'll have my fingerprints taken so as to eliminate them from any forensic evidence I submit. I'm taken to the Commanding Officer's office and asked to take a seat.

Two senior RAOC officers oversee Bomb Disposal activities across the Province. There is the Commanding Officer of 321 EOD Company who is a Major. This is unusual because a CO is normally a Lieutenant Colonel. This chap also holds an appointment called 'SATO' which is an abbreviation for Senior Ammunition Technical Officer.

The second RAOC officer is a Lieutenant Colonel. He is the IEDD adviser to the General Officer Commanding (GOC) British Forces NI. Whilst he doesn't have command responsibility for the unit he holds the appointment of CATO, ie Chief ATO. From time to time he'll issue Standing Operating Procedures that are mandatory for everyone. If you're confused as to who is actually running the ship then you'll just have to read the above for a second or third time.

From the SATO's office I look out over the asphalt square that separates the 321 Portakabin from the more substantial building which is the British Army HQ. Looking back I have just a few moments to contemplate again the guy writing at his desk before he looks up with half a smile on his lips. You know, like a dog just before it bites you. Let's call him JR. He welcomes me to 321. We know each other quite well as we've served together twice before. We also attended the same Pre-Operations IEDD course a couple of months back and it was there that he had sidled over to me to explain that if I should be thinking about medals, which I wasn't, then I should put it out of my mind because, as he put it, 'If the unit puts you up for an award you'll have to answer to me.' Now I happen to think that any soldier is entitled to be affronted by that; having given him no justification for saying it. Me, well frankly I was bemused. It was only when reflecting on it later that I realised I should have taken it more seriously. Anyway I kind of laughed it off and let it go, so today I'm none the wiser as to his reasoning. In case anyone might think he has a sense of humour, then I will say to them that this guy doesn't have a reputation that stretches all that far in that direction. Watching him now across the desk as he looks at me, I wonder if there's more of it to come.

Just a week before I was due to report for this tour of duty my father collapsed at home and died from a heart attack. He was 54 years old and so it came as a great shock to all of us. I was devastated by his loss. My father had no will and my mother didn't even have her own bank account at that time and so urgent financial arrangements had to be made. Probate matters therefore held up my deployment by a few days. Two days after the funeral I reported for duty. I'm probably still in shock. I don't get much sympathy though. Instead, he intimates that the delay in reporting has been a bit of a nuisance; a buggerance factor since the incumbent ATO at Bessbrook will have been inconvenienced, having had to stay on to cover for me. I'm a bit miffed by this because the guy is a mate of mine; I'm sure he was all right with it, and in any case I would have done the same for him.

The SATO doesn't hang around and in his own inimitable way gets to the nub of it; the real ice breaker: 'I told them I don't think you are the right person for Bessbrook.' By 'them' I assume he's referring to the MoD Ammunition Headquarters at Didcot who staff up the NI Operator posts. For a second I think he means that I may not cope with the tour because of my father's death, but then I realise he just thinks I'm not up to the job. It also becomes clear that he thinks I've been promoted to Warrant Officer too soon. Well he's entitled to all these opinions, I guess, but revealing his thoughts to me in this way isn't likely to get us very far up the positive scale.

I don't in any way profess to be an archetypical Bomb Disposal hero such as they are often dramatised by TV and films. Frankly, who does? I'm a fairly average bloke. I don't like heights much and I can't see the point of spiders. I've felt gut-churning fear and I can't say I like it. I certainly don't see myself as brave. I understand the risks and I've simply applied the techniques I've been taught the best I can. I didn't volunteer to carry out this work so it's probably worth mentioning how people of my vintage came to be IEDD Operators in the first place. The fact of the matter is that those of us who signed up as Apprentice Ammunition Technicians in the early to mid 60s only found out about the IEDD element well after we had enlisted. In any case no one could possibly have envisaged the situation in Northern Ireland blowing up in this way, if you'll pardon the pun. Many of us are therefore carrying out IEDD duties more by accident than design. A key point is that in the early days of the Campaign the Ammunition Technicians who carried out these duties were not selected on whether they had an aptitude for it or not. They were a cross-section of types you might see in any profession, who had no choice if they wanted to remain Ammunition Technicians.

Anyway, back to speculating as to what is going on in the SATO's head. Maybe he thinks I haven't got the nerve. Well I think I have and I think I've already proved it. But who really knows where their threshold is? OK, I didn't score especially highly at the IEDD Pre-Ops Exercises. There was one particular mortar job I made a balls of! But I wouldn't be sitting here if the overall results had been too bad.

The SATO gives me the spiel in terms of his expectations but by now I'm distracted and various thoughts tumble around my mind. I'm

The fact of the matter is that those of us who signed up as Apprentice Ammunition Technicians in the early to mid 60s only found out about the IEDD element well after we had enlisted. In any case no one could possibly have envisaged the situation in Northern Ireland blowing up in this way, if you'll pardon the pun. Many of us are therefore carrying out IEDD duties more by accident than design.

thinking, rightly or wrongly, that this guy really doesn't like me and if he doesn't, then it's personal. I'm also thinking that he has a reputation that precedes him among my brethren; metaphorically speaking, he doesn't take prisoners. We know that he's quite ruthless. So I begin to think of the small number of ATO's who have been replaced during the Campaign. None to my knowledge went on to have successful careers as Ammunition Technicians; indeed most had to change profession. All these thoughts make me distinctly uncomfortable. If the matter between us should get out of hand it's likely to be dealt with quickly. We are in an operational theatre after all. No one has time to piss about. If 'push comes to shove' the system we're all signed up to tends to support those who have the seniority. It's part and parcel of the regimental system. This is how I see it anyway. The interview ends.

Fortunately my first encounter with the CATO, Lt Col Chris Hendy, is a much more constructive affair – like normal. He's an upbeat sort of bloke, relaxed in his demeanour and personable, less complicated perhaps, and he doesn't have a reputation that precedes him. He has expectations of me but doesn't have preconceived ideas as to my ability. I come away feeling he's supportive. Frankly it's what I would have expected from any senior officer whose unit is carrying out seriously dangerous operations.

There has always been a tension between those two senior posts. The SATO, as the CO, has command of the unit, but the CATO, who is also located within the 321 HQ, sees himself as ultimately accountable to the GOC for the efficacy of the unit. It could be easy for the two appointments to get in each other's way and I suspect that at times they do.

I'm expected to attend an induction course that will include intelligence and forensic briefings and also explosive demonstrations. I'll

Pre-Operations IEDD Exercise 'Cold Meece'

The Pre-Ops course IEDD exercise is called Exercise Cold Meece. It's named after a village in Staffordshire near to where the exercise originated. The exercise is four days in duration and primarily designed to test Operators and No. 2s in a variety of bomb-related scenarios. The failure rate can be high.

With a lack of any purpose-built facility, the exercise is set in an overgrown, derelict, MoD depot near Grantham. The tests can be taxing, not least because an Operator has first to be able to imagine, for example, that the overgrown track he's standing on is the main street of a town, the crumbling concrete bunker with its smashed windows on his left is a hospital, and the water tower behind him is an oil refinery. The Directing Staff also have personal idiosyncrasies in terms of expectations.

The fear of booby traps can make you too cautious and anyone who fails to consider them sufficiently is penalised for being reckless. Sometimes you wonder how anyone gets through the course at all!

need to return to Lisburn for this at a later date since today is Sunday and Headquarters NI is effectively shut. For now though, at last, I'm on the final leg of my journey to Bessbrook Mill and it's another fast car ride.

Daylight has given way to darkness as the car speeds along. Only a black landscape and oncoming car headlights are discernible. They flash past in a blur for I hardly notice them. My mind is still fixed on the matter that is most likely to have consequences for me. I rationalise the situation, as you do, and a saying jumps into my mind. 'Life's a bitch and then you're dead.'

Well, not me mate, not yet. Life had been too good thus far to be messed up now by someone else. In my mind my priorities are clear; getting home and in one piece and doing a good job that I could be proud of. As I hadn't screwed up in my career just yet, here would be a bad place to start. In fact, and the thought kind of cheers me up, I'm quite looking forward to getting stuck in to the work. If the next four months are going to be a bitch, well at least I'd be mentally prepared for it, I guess.

We arrive in the village of Bessbrook at about 7pm and a few minutes later I get my fist sight of the heavily fortified HQ which I've heard a lot about but never yet seen.

HQ Bessbrook Mill

As with many old mills across the Province, Bessbrook Mill has been turned into a modern version of a fort. It's fenced in with sheets of *wriggly tin*. Ugly grey breeze block sentry posts called sangars have been erected at each entrance and external walls are floodlit at night. The approach to the base has a chicane to prevent vehicle-borne bombs breaking through. There are drills to be followed in the event of a bomb or mortar attack. Across the way is the concreted helicopter port which according to the *Guinness Book of Records* is the busiest in Europe.

Civilians who live nearby will be nervous because we're a target seven days a week and there is often collateral damage from PIRA's attacks. No one can afford to be complacent for the enemy is cunning and persistent, and despite the millions spent obtaining information, surprise is almost always on their side.

How it must be to live out your life and raise a family surrounded by this turmoil is impossible for us to imagine. Soldiers are like tourists. We fly in and a few months later we're out again; back to the relative calm of the mainland. We live in a bubble, separated from the

Operational Headquarters for South Armagh with the busiest heliport in Europe in the foreground.

populace. Outside of the Mill they go about their business the best they can and because the mayhem has been ongoing for so long everyone in the Province will have been touched by it in one way or another.

The Mill contains, I guess, about 600 soldiers; infantry plus a number of supporting echelons like signalmen, search teams, Army Air Corps, logistics and technicians, cooks and intelligence people, Police Liaison Officers. There are probably other specialists that I don't even know about. The regiment has detachments based at Crossmaglen and Newtownhamilton and is supported by another regiment who have a company based at Forkhill. It's quite a lot of soldiers to cover such a relatively small area. My job is to provide specialist IEDD support and advice to all those units and the police as they each carry out their anti-terrorist operations.

Due to the very high probability of attack from ambush bombs, pretty much all roads south of Newry are out of bounds to green vehicles. Most of the jobs I'll be tasked to will be planned in advance, involve helicopter sorties and kick off as dawn breaks. Some will be high-adrenalin races against time but those are likely to be the minority.

I have a team office and our sleeping accommodation is attached. Each member of the team has his own room. The ATOs' section has been here since the beginning so we're fairly comfortable. There's a sofa, soft chairs, TV, video machine, coffee making facilities and a fridge.

> **Wheelbarrow**
>
> The Remote Control Vehicle (RCV) Wheelbarrow is the workhorse developed by the MoD in double quick time to provide Operators with a remote IEDD capability. It's highly versatile as it can carry a variety of equipment, specialist explosives and weaponry that can be deployed against anything really. Its main limitations are the two car batteries it is powered by, which can run out of power when the RCV is at the sharp end, and the 100m umbilical cord that too easily gets trapped or chopped.

Well 'any mug can rough it', as soldiers sometimes say. Our facilities are looked on enviously by the regiments that come and go. We even have a technological miracle provided by the *Sun* newspaper's latest 'Support the Troops' campaign. It's a games consul where the combatants can use a TV screen to play ping pong. It's very popular. Who can say what it'll lead to?

A large map on the wall shows the boundary of our tactical area of responsibility. The map is peppered with colour-coded map pins; each pin is a job. Each colour depicts whether a job turned out to be a Hoax, False Alarm, Live Device, Incendiary, Explosion or a Find. This is how we categorise the outcome of each IEDD task.

With more equipment than most other teams to operate and maintain, I have a second No. 2. So there are four of us in the team – a Corporal Ammunition Technician, a Lance Corporal driver and a Royal Signals, Electronic Counter Measures (ECM) Operator who we affectionally call 'Bleep'. One other, shall we say, more mechanical member of the team is the Remote Control Vehicle (RCV), 'Wheelbarrow Mk. 6'. Wheelbarrow can be expected to take many more risks than I.

Wheelbarrow: the complete equipment schedule.

At the end of the four months I'll be replaced by another second tour Operator. The other members of the team will turnover at the end of their four months. This gradual turnover is called roulement. The infantry units however are replaced en masse at the end of their tour.

As I follow the driver through the corridor complex an Infantry Officer, a Captain, approaches and my driver introduces me. He's the regiment's Adjutant. He smiles broadly, 'Welcome to Bessbrook Felix, good to have you on board.' He calls me Felix because that's the radio code name for the ATO. 321 vehicles have a cat's face emblazoned on them.

He continues, 'Get an early night as we've a body on the border and you're going out at first light . . .'

It's a bit of a shock.

At the office I meet the outgoing ATO, Steve Wilks, and the team; I get introduced and I'm briefed on tomorrow's job. Eventually I get some sleep.

19th January 1981

The body

Shortly after dawn, the outgoing ATO, the team and I, are helicoptered to the border near Jonesborough and we set about the grisly work of recovering the body. The job is made a little easier for us only because he's a member of the Provisional IRA. I'm told he's an informer who's been executed. It seems that the Security Forces received information recently which led to the recovery of a large explosives cache in County Down. It looks as if he's been fingered for it. He was 24 years old.

One dark night hard men abducted him from his house in Belfast. It isn't hard to imagine the fear he must have felt as he was manhandled away to his doom, probably to a lonely farm somewhere near the border. He's interrogated to get a confession and eventually executed with a series of pistol shots. His duffle coat is buttoned up, presumably to keep him together for transportation to the border. He's thrown down and for good measure shots are fired into the back of his head with an Armalite rifle. It's the PIRA mark of a 'tout'. He lies now on a muddy bank a few hundred yards from the border. He's the 170th person to die in South Armagh as a result of the conflict. South Armagh is dubbed 'bandit country' by the Security Forces for good reason.

A dirty war played out for the highest stakes.

In case his body is booby trapped we use the Wheelbarrow to pull him along the road a short distance and away from the immediate area. The ground is searched but nothing untoward is found.

I stand over the guy. His hands are bound with metal wire and he's a bloody mess. This is not the first body I've stood over but it's the first time I've seen someone's brains; they're in the road. It's a sad, sickening end to anybody's life. It's also a sobering re-introduction for me into the brutality of the 'Irish Troubles' and a timely reminder, if ever I needed it, that for PIRA, the Security Forces and especially the Ulster people, this is being played out for the highest stakes.

From the passive to the offensive

We're back from the border by lunchtime and the outgoing ATO and I begin the handover in earnest. Quite naturally since he wants to get home! We walk the Mill and I'm introduced to some of the key people I'll be working with: the infantry Ops Staff, RUC Liaison Officers, Heli Operations, intelligence people, the Royal Engineer Search Team leader; each an expert in his own field and a more cheerful bunch of blokes I have yet to meet.

All our team equipment, weapons and explosives have to be accounted for and signed off. At the explosives store I survey the explosive materials we have at our disposal: plastic explosives, sheet explosives, cutting charges, Disrupter cartridges. There's even a variety of 12-bore shotgun cartridges. It's a far cry from what I would have been looking at just a few years ago.

For anyone in the proximity of a high-order detonation, the effect on the human body is usually catastrophic; shattering. When the dragon roars, the effect is instantaneous; a 'crack' of a sound, not a 'boom'. The white hot gas and heat are expanding at 4,000 metres a second. There isn't time to duck or leap out of the way, no time for evasive action. Anything that can be moved by the blast will be. Anything that will shatter or fragment, will. Anything that can be ripped off, is. Those that have survived the dragon's breath describe it as a white light. If you are far enough away from it the Bomb Disposal Operator's suit will deflect it and if you are too close nothing can save you, for what can shatter metal easily shreds flesh, bone and sinew.

The white hot gas and heat are expanding at 4,000 metres a second. There isn't time to duck or leap out of the way, no time for evasive action. Anything that can be moved by the blast will be. Anything that will shatter or fragment, will. Anything that can be ripped off, is.

Ways have now been developed to utilise those same explosive effects against improvised devices. There's some history and philosophy around IEDD techniques and equipment so it's probably worth explaining it now. An often touted and perhaps traditional view of a Bomb Disposal Operator is of an eccentric but cool head with a steady hand and a briefcase containing various tools; two of which must be a stethoscope and a pair of wire cutters. If this is the picture you have in your head, well it's not too far off the mark should you reflect back to 1966. I emphasise 1966 because this was a big year for Ammunition Technicians serving in Hong Kong. Most people today probably don't realise that Communist elements within Hong Kong tried to destabilise the Province in that year with multiple attacks of crude Improvised Explosive Devices. Ammunition Technicians worked with the Hong Kong police to counter these attacks and thousands of devices were dealt with. Whilst any assumed ability to provide a steady hand is questionable and no one would argue that anyone doing this job is eccentric, by 1966 Operators did have a much bigger box of tricks to play with than simply a set of tools in a satchel or a briefcase. More advanced tools however didn't necessarily make the job any safer. For example, an Operator could call upon an electronic stethoscope so sensitive that placed on a wooden box it could detect the tick of a good watch. This question was asked by an over-enthusiastic student: 'If it is so sensitive to sound, should the bomb go off, wouldn't the noise make you deaf?'

Because an Operator would want to limit any movement of the device he would first secure (ie glue) the suspect package to the ground. For this he used a urethane foam called Coolag. This adhesive is formed by mixing two agents that when brought together foam and then quickly solidify. Once the device was stuck fast he could use a plasma arc torch to produce an intense but localised heat from a 20,000 volt electrical charge. This could cut through thin metal-cased packages. There was even a way to attach the equipment to the package and it would then trepanne a hole in it remotely. Liquid nitrogen was available to be pumped into the package via the hole, which would freeze batteries, stop clockwork mechanisms and solidify any other moving parts. If the bomb had not gone off at this point in the proceedings and you were therefore still around, you might now be in a good position to snip away at the key components. At which point the legendary wire cutters would come into their own.

An armoured screen on wheels was also developed that could be pushed to the target, keeping the screen between the device and the Operator. A long-handled shovel pushed through a hole could be used to manipulate and even lift the device away from the intended target. I know all this because this was the equipment I was taught to use at my first IEDD course in 1970. At the time I have to say it all seemed rather reasonable and quite exciting.

These inadequate Render Safe strategies together with this perverse way of thinking were initially carried forward into the NI Campaign.

Whilst a number of Operators were injured in the Hong Kong Campaign it is quite amazing that we lost only one, Sergeant Charles Workman. He bled to death on a ledge after being blown over a cliff by the force of an explosion. The survival rate was higher in Hong Kong partly because the bomb makers used only gunpowders, or low explosives as they're called, rather than high explosives.

The shortcomings of all the IEDD equipment in those days can be summarised as its passive and less than offensive nature and the time it takes to deploy it. Not to mention the number of times the device has to be approached by the Operator. We used up time trying to confirm whether a device was actually real or not and then spent an awful lot of time in the danger area. These inadequate Render Safe strategies together with this perverse way of thinking were initially carried forward into the NI Campaign.

A big difference between the Hong Kong emergency and the NI campaign was not least the significant amounts and types of explosives the NI terrorists had access to. Another was the technology available to PIRA. British Telecom components discovered in early Irish devices and the sophistication in the types of switching used suggested that technicians with a BT-type background were building them. The device circuitry was often complex, incorporating multiple switching arrangements. Sometimes what the Operator could easily get his hands on is what they wanted him to touch, move or cut.

The more passive approach to IEDD almost certainly contributed to the death of the first Operator, Capt Stewardson. He attempted to gain access to a plywood container via the lid after having secured the device to the ground using the Coolag mixture. X-rays taken of similar devices later showed that a clever method of switching had been used by the bomber. Cutting into devices by hand, and chopping wires as an initial action, quickly became a no-no. Even so the passive approach to dealing with devices was perpetuated. When for example it was discovered that detergent foam could disperse the fireball and heat from an explosion, thereby significantly reducing the blast effects, an armoured Humber vehicle (called a Pig) was adapted to dispense foam over devices. This technique was especially used in Belfast from 1973 through to 1977 mainly to combat car bombs. Whilst there is no doubt it worked when it worked, when it didn't work, because for example the bomb didn't function or it was a false alarm, then the whole city was tied up for hours and hours. And if, as happened at least once, an Operator made a manual approach into the foam, he could become completely disorientated in the white-out and lost, which is a bit disconcerting when you assume you are in the vicinity of a large car bomb.

And if, as happened at least once, an Operator made a manual approach into the foam, he could become completely disorientated in the white-out and lost, which is a bit disconcerting when you assume you are in the vicinity of a large car bomb.

Another piece of kit was put forward by the BBC *World in Action* team. They came to the Army School of Ammunition, when it was located at Bramley in Hampshire, to test out a specialist blanket that someone had invented. It was supposed to be capable of suppressing an explosive blast. As the slow motion cameras demonstrated, it could, more or less, but as was pointed out at the time the main problem with this idea is that someone has to place the blanket on the device in the first place and if the device doesn't go off, someone has to lift it off – any volunteers? Some people must think this is what Operators are paid to do!

I remember one of my earlier Northern Ireland Pre-Ops courses. The training area was littered with derelict cars on which Operators

The Foaming Pig in action: Belfast, circa 1974.

practised their access techniques. We had a special punch that when pressed against the windscreen could shatter it, a technique for removing windscreens all in one piece and a type of can opener with which car body panels could be opened up like a tin of beans. I mean, it was good fun wrecking cars during courses but it wasn't anything like as funny using the techniques for real.

Portable X-ray machines were quickly developed, which also perpetuated the passive approach. But these X-Ray equipments were not small and an early design required two men to lift it to the target – any volunteers? In the interim Operators were provided with what we called, the 'Gamma Bomb'. Placing this 30lb lump of lead in front of the device and opening it up at the front exposed an iridium radioactive source that emitted gamma rays. These have the same effect on film as X-rays and would provide us with a similar picture of the contents. The risks associated with radioactive materials were real, and one more thing that can be added to the list that will probably jeopardise the health of some Operators in the years to come.

The deployment of many of these pieces of equipment overlapped so it's difficult to say now exactly when the policy changed to much more offensive IEDD techniques. In fact even in the early days, as a form of self preservation I guess, Operators were beginning to use home-made explosive strips and explosive charges to gain access to devices. It makes me shudder today but I once read the SATO's comments in an IEDD report from that time which required the Operator to think seriously about sandbagging a device so as to reduce the likelihood of collateral damage occurring should the device function whilst he was taking that type of IEDD action!

I'm glad to say things had moved on by the time I carried out my first tour as an Operator in 1975. *Disruption* became the byword for IEDD and this is now synonymous with the term Controlled Explosion that everyone hears about. The applied principle is: Why waste time and sweat trying to confirm if something is a device or not, thereby endangering yourself and providing the device with space in which to function? Get in quickly and do something about it immediately. If it turns out not to have been a device, well, so what? If you can reduce its effect, great. The most important thing is that any people at risk are evacuated and kept safe.

IEDD weaponry these days is capable of smashing electrical circuits before the explosives can be initiated. At the same time the penetrative and disruptive effects of these weapons expose and thereby provide access to the device components. Some of the weapons are so extreme they have as yet not been approved for use on the UK mainland. In 1974 we had what was called the Beguine: a heavy 10-inch square metal plate which was projected at the device in the vertical plane by a high explosive charge. The plate was held in a wooden cassette fitted to a lightweight metal frame that could be deployed with the Wheelbarrow. Trouble was, it could easily be tangled up in the cables and the plate was often deflected. If that wasn't violent enough we were issued with an 84mm Carl Gustav anti-tank gun: a weapon which is primarily designed to take out a main battle tank. Normally fired from the shoulder, when deployed for IEDD purposes it was fitted in a stand. Solid non high explosive rounds were fired to disrupt vehicle-borne devices. As mentioned earlier I used the equipment in 1976, firing two rounds at a truck full of mortars. It was a bloody dangerous tool, not least because a projectile like that isn't easily stopped by the cab of a truck! The thinking behind its use is clearly a long way along the road from Hong Kong.

The pigstick: second to none for sledging packages.

Vehicle disruption became the name of the game. A spinning beer keg spews out its lethal guts.

Opening it all up in one go is only the beginning for the Operator . . .

The flatsword: second to none for sledging milk churns and beer kegs.

84mm Anti-tank gun Carl Gustav. I'm lining up the bore sight on a Leyland truck full of mortars. The two rounds fired disrupted the electric firing leads, but christ knows where they landed.

22nd January 1981

Hoax, Monaghan Street, Newry

The outgoing ATO has left and having been given a few days to settle in, at 09.00hrs I'm tasked to deal with an incident at a garage in Monaghan Street. A milk churn with a plastic bag taped around the rim has been discovered by the key holder of a garage. I send in the Wheelbarrow.

One shot with a Disrupter into the opening reveals that it's a hoax device comprised of an alarm clock, some wiring and a lump of putty. It's all been very straightforward for us. I declare the device clear and everything around about quickly gets back to normal.

We'll never know the ulterior motive for wasting our time. One theory is that they want to know our patterns so they are observing us/me.

A hoax. Why? For what reason?

Hoax components. Putting the frighteners on somebody or perhaps they're clocking us.

23rd January 1981

Beer keg device, Belfast to Dundalk railway line

Next day I'm in a chopper and when it banks steeply I'm able to get a good look at the main Belfast to Dundalk railway line in the vicinity of Newtown. The railway is closed after a call to the Samaritans has said there are three devices on the railway line. A beer keg has since been spotted lying between the tracks. The helicopter pilot speaks to me. He's convinced that a Guinness barrel has fallen off a train. I don't share his thought. I mean, how many barrels of beer fall off trains? Isn't it every bloke's unrequited dream? Beer kegs, like milk churns, are often used by PIRA in their explosive devices so there's a job for us here. The railway won't open again until it's cleared.

The job is all about teamwork. A great lineup and I probably never really thanked them enough.

L. to R. Turner, Walker, Wharton, Wicks.

All our equipments, including two of our vehicles, are heli portable. It's the safest way to get around South Armagh.

The beer keg device. It isn't just about the device you can see . . .

There's a lot to think about at an incident not least because the Operator is also responsible for everyone else's safety. In the first place there's a need to get a grip on the scenario and untangle it. Magic is most helpful at times like these because an early all-important question is: What might the terrorist want to achieve by this attack? This exercise provides a list of likely options and combinations which depending on your imagination can be very long or very short. By weighing the probabilities of each you are better placed to manage the inherent risks. It's therefore important to get as much information as possible on how the incident materialised. In this case however there isn't any additional information except that every so often PIRA attack the railway and the bridges for which they're guaranteed publicity. The lack of information and the time the terrorist might have taken to plan it means we do have to be very careful since the list of options might be considered long.

There's a lot to think about at an incident not least because the Operator is also responsible for everyone else's safety. In the first place there's a need to get a grip on the scenario and untangle it.

Agreeing tactics with the 1QLR Company Commander Major Scrace. 'Magic', a member of WIS, is in the foreground.

Eyeballing the beer keg from a relatively safe distance prior to rendering it safe. 60lb of home-made explosives would have made a real mess of the railway.

The Infantry make the area secure and the Royal Engineers carry out their searches. Eventually we get on the ground. I need to eyeball the device so taking the binoculars I scramble up the grassy bank over the fence into the adjacent field. Moving closer using the ground as cover I get to within 30–40 metres of it. With the binoculars I can see clearly that the top of the keg has been machined open and a plastic fertiliser sack is stuffed into the opening. A plywood Time and Power Unit (TPU) is lying next to the keg. The TPU provides the bomber with safety in arming and a time delay before the device functions. PIRA have come a long way since 1973 when 38 of their operatives blew themselves up with their own bombs. Such a timer would normally have only a couple of hours to run, max, so it looks as if the device has failed to function. Tracing the electrical leads I can see that a detonator is taped to the white detonating cord (or Det Cord as we call it) which is protruding from the centre of the keg. The layman might think this is plastic clothes line but it contains a core of high explosive and is used extensively in demolitions or quarrying for linking explosives together.

So is the device safe? Well, let's think about it. We might assume the bomber tested the batteries before he set out. If not they could be flat. But perhaps the electrical contacts are contaminated. If so a speck of dust or corrosion might be holding them fractionally apart. The smallest jolt is all that's needed for the circuit to close and the device to function. It's also hazardous because static electricity has been known to initiate electrical detonators and here we have the electrical leads almost touching the batteries.

I pass a soldier who has been far closer to the device than was good for him. He tells me he thinks it's a dud. I thank him for his intuition and advice . . .

Three devices were reported but this information can be taken with a hefty pinch of salt. There are any number of possibilities to consider, one of which is that the keg is in fact a decoy and the real device is hidden somewhere else in the vicinity. Another is that the keg doesn't actually have a timer at all but something more sinister; perhaps it's radio controlled. I'm thinking of multiple scenarios and the likelihood of each as I crawl away from the grassy bank and make my way back to the Control Point.

I have the RCV Wheelbarrow slung under a Wessex helicopter and the pilot lifts it from the field down in between the tracks. We also lift onto the tracks our heli portable vehicle to provide us with some cover. The RCV is then tooled up with two IEDD Disrupters and the Browning semi-automatic shotgun. The latter is loaded with a mixture of shot. The Disrupter is a weapon designed to penetrate certain types of containers and shatter components and circuitry before the detonator can be initiated. The shotgun is good for smashing up components and chopping wires.

We set the Wheelbarrow on its way between the right-hand pair of rails, eyeballing its direction of travel. The No. 2 flicks the switch on the control box that stops the left track for a second and allows the machine to straighten up. Then, because he's over-compensated, it's a sharp flick on the right switch. Then it's both tracks forward and away it goes, up and over, up and over each concrete sleeper until it's in the vicinity of the target. Then it's all eyes to the CCTV monitor. He brings the RCV up close to the main target: the TPU. Then by extending the boom over the track he brings the Disrupter up close to the TPU, inching forward until the Disrupter is almost touching it. Then stop. I say, 'OK, let's do it.'

A warning is passed to all troops to expect a controlled explosion. It's fingers in the ears time in case it doesn't quite go according to plan and all eyes are on the CCTV monitor. '*Boom.*' The sound is akin to a shotgun blast and the TPU disintegrates. It's overkill frankly but I don't have a smaller weapon in the armoury that is as reliable. We use the Wheelbarrow to roll the keg around a bit and up-end it. This movement doesn't eliminate everything. I still need to see inside the keg. The only quick and safe way of doing this is to cut the keg in half.

Controlled explosion on the firing mechanism. Wheelbarrow at its best.

Gone are the days when a hacksaw might have had to be considered. Today we have a specialist explosive weapon called Flatsword. It's a hardened metal blade contained in a large wooden cassette. It's cumbersome and heavy and the blade is projected by a kilogram of military high explosive. The weapon isn't something we're encouraged to use in built-up areas or back on the UK mainland even. But out here in the open there's little chance of collateral damage. Because of the rough terrain the cassette would fall apart if we tried to deliver it using the RCV, so I have to carry it to the device myself.

The weapon is fitted into its frame and primed with the sheet explosives. An electric detonator is connected to a twin flex cable and inserted into the plastic receptor. Lifting the weapon and pointing it forward I begin the perilous journey to the target. It's perilous mainly because with the weight of the cassette, the uneven ground and the clumsy suit I'm likely to stumble and break my bloody leg before I even get to the target. Safety conscious as I am though, I have the weapon facing forward and the satisfaction of knowing that if the weapon should function prematurely I will not be cut in half. The IEDD suit would in this case be helpful but only in reducing the effort of those who would have to recover me, since what would remain would be big pieces.

My heavy breathing soon steams up the visor. I can only vaguely make out the beer keg in the middle distance and I can't see anything immediately in front of me. Then, within 20ft of the keg, I'm yanked to a halt. It's fortunate that my end of the cable is tied to the metal frame otherwise the force would have ripped out the detonator. The electrical twin flex cable is being fed out from a reel back at the Control Point. I curse and turn back to see what's going on. Frantic efforts are being made to sort it out. The cable, as it is apt to do if one takes one's eyes off it, has unravelled too quickly and tangled itself around the reel. But whilst they wrestle with the problem I'm left standing a few feet short of the device and well within the danger area. I place the weapon on the ground and push up the visor to shout at the team. 'Lift up the reel and come forward with it.' One of the guys signals that he's understood and I turn back to the job in hand. I don't bother to pull the visor down this time. As the No. 2 carries the reel forward with its tangled cable, I haul the weapon the last few feet to the target. I position the stand so that the forward part of the cassette is within a few inches of the beer keg. I don't have to mess about with the height as we have it set about right.

Back at the Control Point now the electronic firing switch is connected to the unjammed firing cable and primed by the No. 2. I give a warning to the ground troops and for everyone local to get under cover. Then on the shout, 'Firing!' the buttons are pressed and 'Bang!'

The controlled explosion is much more substantial this time. As the smoke dissipates we can see that the metal container has been cut neatly in two. The bottom half looks as if it hasn't moved.

I give it a minute or so and then walk back up to it. Two types of home-made explosives are spread about. Together they weigh about 60lb. Nothing else of a sinister nature is evident. We bag up the forensics, clear down and move out. The railway is unscathed and will quickly get back to normal.

Had the device functioned it would have produced a bloody great hole in the ground, taking out all four rails and possibly the adjacent bridge. All this would have completely messed up the BR timetable for a week or so at least.

Looking about me as the lads pack up I'm conscious that it's only when we finish and leave the area that so can the infantry. I may be here to support them but they're fundamental to my team's security. If I take two or three days over a job, which can happen, then it's the infantry who have to stay out in the freezing fields to maintain the cordon. I decide that within reason I'll try and speed up my side of any clearance operations. With 'within reason' underlined. The alternative is to pay slavish attention to our Render Safe Procedures. Although they err on the side of safety, and we have them for a very good reason, they can massively increase the time taken to complete an operation.

Applying our procedures pedantically just as they are written without too much thought takes you into the realm of the trained monkey. The RSPs will get you there, but not anytime soon. Sometimes the threat can be over-egged and an Operator can be too cautious. Like many things in life there is a balance to be found. This is no different in that respect.

Applying our procedures pedantically just as they are written without too much thought takes you into the realm of the trained monkey. The RSPs will get you there, but not anytime soon.

26th January 1981

Explosion, Golden Griddle Restaurant, Newry

In the intervening period I'm called to deal with two minor incidents. One is the discovery of an army rifle grenade which was reported lost by a foot patrol a long time ago. Lost equipment when found is a real headache because you can never be sure it hasn't been tampered with. I destroy it in a controlled explosion. The second is an army torch, also lost and now found and feared to be booby trapped. I X-ray it. It isn't.

At 18.20hrs on 26th January I'm tasked to an incident in Newry. At 18.00hrs three women were present in the Golden Griddle restaurant in Sandy Street when two armed men shouting 'IRA' entered it and placed a blue holdall next to the counter. The bomb hasn't gone off yet and as we can deploy by vehicle there's a lot of urgency. Using the wall map we pinpoint the street and quickly decide on a route in. Now we're moving as fast as possible. Everyone knows the drill; no orders need to be given. The adrenalin flows as I jog down the corridor towards the courtyard. At the same time I'm fastening my flack jacket and the chin strap on my crash helmet. A crash-out like this may be the norm for teams in Belfast or Londonderry but for us it's the exception. 'Good luck Felix,' I hear someone say. The Transit is already moving by the time I get to it. Hauling open the door I leap into the front seat and inadvertently crash the clumsy helmet against the door jamb. I curse. The blue lights are on as we roar out of the Mill past the entrance sangar. I don't see any of it because my head is down logging the incident in my note book. I don't feel fear, only excitement.

I reckon we're about half way there when the radio bursts into life and Bessbrook Ops speaks to us. 'Hello 45 Echo, this is Zero. Rucksack at the scene have reported that the device has functioned. Over.'

'Bollocks!' I shout before responding in my best radio voice. '45 Echo. OK, thanks, we'll be at the task location in about 10 minutes. Out.'

It's an anticlimax; we're all disappointed. I feel the adrenalin and the excitement subsiding. At the scene the RUC are with the owner of the restaurant – one of the ladies present when the bombers burst in. The restaurant hasn't caught fire. I listen to her story and then have a look inside. The restaurant is a mess consistent with about 4–5kg of HME. I declare the area clear. Understandably the lady is upset but she tries to hide it. I find parts of a CO_2 gas cylinder which substantiates my estimation. The only real casualty is the owner's cat whose curiosity has sadly been its undoing.

27th January 1981

Explosion, railway line, Meigh

At 21.00hrs I'm notified that the main Belfast to Dundalk railway line has been attacked again. I'm also notified that the Killeavy Truck Company, a vehicle yard adjacent to the railway, has been destroyed by fire and explosion. Both attacks have obviously been carried out by the same PIRA unit. It's their way of making up for the failed beer keg attack four days earlier. I guess we're dealing with people who take things very personally.

We deploy next day to the railway line and I get on the ground late at about 14.00hrs. I find that one rail is very severely bent and twisted. Under this is a relatively small crater, the seat of the explosion. The damage is consistent with about 2–3kg of commercial explosive. I declare the area clear. This is always a risky call because you can only really declare something safe that you can see and evaluate. The fact that nothing else is found doesn't always mean something isn't there, lurking, poised to catch you out. There's only so much that can be searched.

It's too late to begin the vehicle yard investigation so the job is postponed until tomorrow. As light fades we're extracted by helicopter back to Bessbrook.

28th January 1981

Blast incendiary, Killeavy Truck Company

Trucks burnt out, cabs and dashboards melted like giant candles. It must have been a regular fireworks display.

Next day we're back on the scene. I decide not to bring the Wheelbarrow as I think we're only investigating a series of explosions. The Wheelbarrow would have to be transported on one of our two heli portable vehicles and moving all this around the countryside via helicopter is a bit of a logistics exercise.

The large metal gates at the entrance of the truck company are wide open. It's a big yard full of machinery, large trucks and tankers. Everything has cooled down nicely and there's no sign of the fires that must have raged two nights before. Just about all the equipment and trucks are burnt out; an insurance write-off. Truck cabs are melted like large wax candles. I can see some lightweight buildings which I assume are the offices and workshops. They appear unscathed.

I set up our Control Point just outside the entrance. The Royal Engineer Searchers do their job and sweep through the whole area, reporting the seats of many explosions as they go. Then I get news that one of the searchers has discovered an unexploded device in the cab of a large truck. He describes it as a one gallon Jeyes fluid can which has a metal-cased explosive charge taped to it. On the cab floor, adjacent to the can, is a plywood TPU. The device is a blast incendiary. A gallon of petrol detonated in this way is quite spectacular. All of a sudden the job takes on a wholly different complexion.

I contemplate the IEDD suit. It's heavy, comprised as it is of very many laminated nylon sheets. It does have its uses, for example it will save me from the blast should the small cased charge detonate. It will also reduce the effects of exploding petrol. Most importantly it will keep me warm as it's bloody freezing. Better on than off then!

I step into the trousers first. These are held up by cotton tape braces which are tied in a bow across my chest. The backs of the leg are zipped up. I put my hands into the heavy jacket with its thick collar and this is again zipped up at the rear. Two large makrolon armoured plates are inserted into pockets in the front of the jacket. There are gloves but no one wears them because of the loss of dexterity. The helmet is very heavy with its thick plastic visor so I elect instead to wear a lightweight visored crash helmet which is much less cumbersome and doesn't steam up quite as quickly. The suit manufacturers will say that wearing a lightweight helmet completely negates the effectiveness of the suit. I'm sure they're right, but I'll take my chances. Taking a Disrupter, a 'hook and line', and also the Pentax 35mm camera I approach the device.

I don't see that I'm up against the clock here as the time will have long expired on the type of clockwork timer PIRA uses. Of course there is always the chance that you are being confronted by a new innovation or a new technology. This is what makes the work unpredictable.

The door of the vehicle is open and peering around it I see that the device stands on the cab floor in the passenger well. It's at my head height. Everything about the device is as described except for one other thing, which is odd. The dowel pin, by which the device is normally armed, is still in place. Odd things are always highly suspicious and I'm a lot less comfortable now than I was five minutes ago.

The blast incendiary – a device with an odd secret.

Separating out the components with a pair of wire cutters.

Does it mean the device is safe, ie unarmed? Well it would be madness to assume it was. There is every possibility that the can in fact contains a separate device with an anti-lift switch incorporated. If so the device will function when it's moved a few millimetres. PIRA have used this type of booby trap in the past with tragic consequences for one of our Operators. I take a photograph of the device and then get on with the job.

Ideally I'd destroy the TPU with the Disrupter and take out the can at the same time. Unfortunately there's insufficient room to position the long metal tube without a risk of disturbing the device. Where is the Wheelbarrow when I need it! I elect instead to 'hoik' the device out to somewhere I can get at it and for this I'll use the ubiquitous 'hook and line'. This may seem to be a passive way of dealing with it but we need to get the job done and get out. I'm conscious that an awful lot of soldiers are tied up in an operation protecting a pile of burned-out trucks.

I take a deep breath and very gingerly place the line around the device and then back off.

Back at the Control Point and breathing again I gently take up the slack in the rope. Pulling on the rope I hear the device hit the ground with a dull clunk. This tells me the can is full of something or other. The device might have gone off at that point but has chosen not to. I leave it for a short period, a 'secondary soak' as we say, before approaching it once again with the Disrupter.

I don't need it. The components are spread over the ground. If you can't always be careful in this job at the very least you need to be lucky. The lid of the TPU has detached itself and the entire electrical circuit is visible. Examining it I can see that the TPU has in fact been rewired. The clothes peg arming switch is no longer in the firing circuit. This means

Recovering the remains of the devices for the forensic lab.

that the device was always armed despite the dowel pin and should have functioned when the timer ran out. It will be for the Forensic Science Lab to determine why the device failed to function.

Petrol is leaking out of the can. I check the base of it for anything untoward: it's clear. Using a Stanley knife I cut the tape that secures the cased charge to the can and then with a pair of wire cutters I separate the cased charge from the TPU and tape up the ends of each wire. The device is effectively neutralised now. I take the bits back to the Control Point and we bag them up. All except the cased charge. This could be unstable and therefore isn't transportable. For evidential purposes I take an X-ray of its inner workings with my portable X-ray equipment and then destroy it in a small controlled explosion.

As was touched on earlier, at the beginning of the NI Campaign the X-ray equipment was considered very much a prime bit of kit. The RSP then would be to X-ray the object in order to confirm it was a

Checking out the rest of the damage.

device before tackling it. Today the facility is still used, but primarily to confirm the contents of an object once any associated hazards have been dealt with. The equipment I have with me now is like an elongated squared off torch that I can carry with one hand. We also use Polaroid film, thus dispensing with tins of developer and fixer. These days it's all nice and tidy.

Whilst the lads pack up I go on to examine the remainder of the yard. A mixture of blast incendiaries and gas cylinder type devices have indeed been used; a total of ten in all. It must have been quite a fireworks display. The fragments of gas cylinders and metal cans are collected and bagged up for Forensics, job done, and it's back to Bessbrook.

However, this task doesn't actually end here. There's a postscript. At 9pm that evening I'm called to a discussion at the Ops room. A torch has subsequently been discovered on a tanker at the vehicle yard. No one admits to owning it and so it will have to be cleared. The problem is that because the area is well within bandit country a second fully fledged clearance operation would have to be mounted. No one wants that. A plan is therefore devised that would get the job done with the minimum number of troops.

The Close Observation Platoon (COP) is a group of soldiers who carry out specialist covert and surveillance operations. They are going to form a protection party for me and my No. 2. We'll use two civilian, ie covert, cars, so it's civilian clothes. My No. 2 and I will be in the first car with two armed escorts. We'll travel in convoy through deepest South Armagh to arrive at the end of the lane where the vehicle yard is located. Our car will then drive forward to the yard and my No. 2 and I will leap out with our IEDD equipment. The car will then drive on to the other end of the lane and the soldiers will cordon and secure it. The soldiers in the other car will already have secured the other end of the lane. We expect to be in and out of there in 15 minutes. It all sounds simple but that is the way of it, with plans.

Our car screeches to a halt. The two of us leap out with our hands full of equipment. The car roars off into the darkness. It's silent. It's also pitch black; I can't see a bloody thing. I run to where I think the yard is, straight into the gate. Crash! I have a gate imprinted on my face. 'Jesus, we're locked out!' I whisper.

As my eyes become accustomed to the darkness I see that the owners have rebuilt the perimeter fence and closed and padlocked the large gates for good measure. We don't have a radio to tell anyone this, so by the time our vehicle comes to collect us we're still trying to get over the fence. 'Have you finished?' hisses the voice of impatience from somewhere behind and below me. 'I haven't f*****g started,' I hiss back. 'Can you give us a bloody hand?"

He dumps his Armalite and gets stuck in. I swear it's like a Laurel and Hardy movie. You couldn't make it up. Looking into the yard from the top of the fence I can see that if I do eventually get in I probably won't be able to get out again. Brilliant! Also nagging at me is the thought that this is the stamping ground of some really nasty bad guys. Them turning up isn't completely in the realms of fantasy. If they do, I think, there is every possibility they will laugh themselves to death!

I finally get over the fence using the gate pillar and eventually locate the torch which is on the horizontal ladder along the top of a tanker. It's an army torch. One of the search team members has probably left it behind – maybe.

I can't easily position the X-ray equipment so I elect instead to tumble the torch off the tanker with the hook and line. Down it comes with a thump. I lift it. The weight is spot on. I take a chance and open it up from the front, removing the bulb and reflector. It's clear.

After another 10 minutes scrambling back up the fence with half the COP helping, we're out of there.

It wasn't the best executed operation or RSP I'd ever been party to, but it had to have been the funniest!

It wasn't the best executed operation or RSP I'd ever been party to, but it had to have been the funniest!

30th January 1981

Derrybeg Community Centre – a riotous assembly

Over the next couple of days I deal with two more incidents in Newry. One is the routine clearance of a stolen car spotted in a housing estate. The other involves two suspicious devices discovered at the Derrybeg Community Centre. As regards the latter, it's late evening when they're reported and troops are reluctant to go into this housing estate at night in case it's a trap – a 'come on' situation. The job is therefore left until next day.

Next morning we're at the scene and I quickly come to accept the army view of the estate. Whilst I'm working to clear the devices, soldiers on the outer cordon find themselves having to contain a small riot. This wasn't anticipated so the troops don't have the proper gear to defend themselves. A car is set on fire. There's a lot of shouting and stick waving. The cordon doesn't look especially secure and is never too far from collapsing. I keep one eye on all that is happening behind me since I'm obliged to abandon the task if my team's protection can't be guaranteed. Neither I nor the team are trained in riot drills so if anyone nasty does get too close they're likely to get much more than they bargained for. Anybody who has seen close up, or has been involved in a riot will testify that behaviour can quickly transmogrify into the grotesque and lead to unforeseen and tragic consequences, especially if the situation is underestimated and control is lost. These thoughts incentivise me into not hanging about. Two items in our IEDD equipment schedule are semi-automatic shotguns – one of which is sawn off. I keep the latter close to hand having concluded that if 'push comes to shove' and I have to invite someone to make my day, it will be a much more useful deterrent than my 9mm Browning pistol.

In short time, cutting one or two corners, I discover that both devices are hoaxes. I conclude that they have in all likelihood been planted by the youths outside who wished to get troops into the area for some sport. In the event everyone gets out in one piece and the Derrybeg Community centre is left unscathed.

3rd February 1981

Ambush Device, Chancellors Road, Bessbrook

Three days later at 15.20hrs the wall mounted plastic intercom by my bed bursts in to life. 'Can you come through to the Ops room Felix?' It's more of a command than a question.

'Certainly sir,' says I. Such calls generally mean business.

A group of people await my arrival. The duty Ops Officer is accompanied by two policemen and a civilian. 'Felix,' says the Ops Officer, 'this is Mr X. He works for the Council. Earlier today, while clearing debris from culverts on the Chancellors Road, he came across a number of milk churns in one of them.'

Culverts

Ireland is green and wet because an awful lot of weather comes in off the Atlantic. It is also a terrain of undulating hills and lakes and is therefore criss-crossed by a great many streams.

Wherever a stream comes up against a road, a tunnel has to be constructed to allow the stream through. There are thousands of these. PIRA realised early on that culverts are ideal for concealing large ambush bombs and many members of the Security Forces have come to grief from this form of attack.

I speak with the guy. He thinks there are three churns. There isn't much else he can tell me as he didn't hang around!

The senior Police Officer takes me to one side and continues. 'This coincides with three telephone calls we've received over the last 10 days stating that a farm was on fire in that area. On each occasion a covert police car responded but no fire was found. We considered the calls hoaxes.'

It didn't need a brain surgeon to work out that PIRA had tried to entice the police into the area with the intention of detonating the device as their car passed over it. It hadn't happened only because the bomber had been unable to identify the police vehicle. Fortunately no military vehicle had used that road recently. The road is now out of bounds to all Security Forces.

A helicopter is called up and we reconnoitre the area. I'm accompanied by a Company Commander who will be in overall charge of the operation and also the Royal Engineers Search Adviser. All of us need to see the lie of the land for our differing purposes.

The helicopter circles the culvert and I peer down. There's a stone parapet directly opposite a white gated driveway. I can see the culvert entrance which is about 4ft high. It's quite well concealed from the road as it's surrounded by hedges. It's not so easy though to see the stream's route up to where it runs into the culvert. I also take this opportunity to look for an area that will make a suitable Control Point. Not too close, not too far away. And because of what I will have to do, I need a straight run at it.

A culvert with a deadly secret.

Next day, at first light, the infantry move into the area and dig in. The surrounding high ground is dominated, the roads are sealed off, traffic is diverted and a cordon is put in place.

Once the area is declared secure, the Royal Engineer Search team of the Parachute Regiment go in. Using their electronic detection equipment and sniffer dogs they sweep the hedges and road for any additional devices. They also search our landing site. This work can be very risky since a searcher won't detect a device until they are pretty much upon it.

All the equipment I require is packed onto 'Gobbler'. Who gave it this code name I do not know. It's a Land-Rover, but you wouldn't recognise it as such. It's stripped down to the very basics to make it heli portable. The Wheelbarrow stays behind again. Despite having tracks it doesn't work particularly well on rough ground. In any case this job is going to require a number of manual approaches.

I've selected a landing site about 400 metres from the culvert and this is where the helicopters deposit us. We leap out and release the under-slung vehicle from the second chopper. The din from the helicopter engines is deafening, its impossible to speak and hand signals are the order of the day. It's a relief when they finally lift off and roar away into the grey sky. Silence and tranquillity descend again on another wet, muddy field. At least it's not raining. Anybody else might think the area is picturesque, but for now it's too cold to even notice it and there is far too much to do.

I look around me at the hedges and ground. It's a nervous time because even at this early juncture we're trying to outthink the terrorist. If they've second guessed our landing site we could already be in trouble.

Because our ropes and cables are only so long we need to be much nearer to the target. We move forward to the agreed Control Point about 80 metres from the culvert. We're perilously close if the device should function for there's an awful lot of heavy stuff to be flung into the air and precious little cover.

The RE Search Adviser (RESA), a Staff Sergeant, approaches me. His men have discovered the twin flex Command Wire that was to have detonated the device. It's been laid above ground and enters the culvert from the far side.

A safety procedure is that I chop the Command Wire before making an approach to the culvert, thus isolating the terrorist firing point from the device. I take the red explosives box, a firing cable and some other equipment and with my No. 2 follow the Search Adviser down to the road, giving the culvert a wide berth.

No real attempt has been made to conceal the cable and it follows a line of hedgerows towards the top of the ridge line about 300m from the culvert.

Everything we do in IEDD, we try to do remotely. This is no exception. Attaching a small explosive charge to the twin flex I run out a firing cable and then fire it. The bang echoes all around the hills. If the locals didn't know we were here before, they do now. I test the electrical circuit in both directions. There's a circuit at the culvert end which tells me that a detonator is connected and the device is primed. The circuit is open at the other end. If I'd found this to be the other way around, then the job would have become even more interesting. That is on the basis that you don't really want to live in interesting times.

There's a circuit at the culvert end which tells me that a detonator is connected and the device is primed. The circuit is open at the other end. If I'd found this to be the other way around, then the job would have become even more interesting. That is on the basis that you don't really want to live in interesting times.

The search teams have now located the terrorist firing point and report that a large blue battery pack is lying in the grass there. I'll deal with that later; the culvert is the priority. We get back to the Control Point across the other side of the road and make the final arrangements. In particular, the Electronic Counter Measures equipment is switched on and warmed up. The RF output will provide me with an electronic safety umbrella against the current range of radio controlled devices. At least that's what we're taught. Everything is now set and I can't put off the inevitable any longer. I grasp the end of our car tow rope. It's strong and it needs to be, for one milk churn full of home-made explosives will weigh at least 100lb (50 kilos) and I'm going to use this rope to drag the churns out of the culvert. I put the 35mm Pentax camera in my pocket along with a pair of wire cutters and a Stanley knife. I also take with me a primed Disrupter in case I come across something unexpected that I could use it on. I don't wear the IEDD suit as it's far too cumbersome and in any case won't be much use if anything goes wrong. Then I'm on my way. Someone says good luck. Team members pay out the cables from the reels and I take that lonely path up to the culvert entrance. At this point I have to believe we've done everything we can to reduce the risks in my favour but you never really know what you're dealing with until afterwards. For example the milk churns might even be a decoy and I'm approaching the culvert exactly how the terrorist might have assumed I would. It's a nervy time.

Arriving at the entrance I look around for anything out of the ordinary: wires, disturbed earth etc. I feel my heart thumping. I'm not cold any more. I take a deep breath and drop down off the concrete retaining wall into the shallow stream with a splash. The only noise now is my laboured breathing and the seemingly magnified twittering of a bird somewhere nearby. I look into the culvert. It's fairly gloomy but as my eyes accustom to it I can see there are far more than the three milk churns I was told about. I count six, maybe seven. There is probably a quarter of a ton of high explosives. I'm not overly alarmed because from where I'm standing it doesn't make much difference.

A quarter of a ton of explosives in seven milk churns.

I set the camera shutter to a low speed so as not to use the flash and take a photograph. If it doesn't work out there may at least be a record of what it looked like for others to mull over. I don't dwell on the reality which is that if the device does function, the crater would be massive and the camera would probably be dust – like me.

Leaving both the camera and Disrupter behind on the grass bank and with a sense of dread I crawl up the cold stone tunnel on all fours, dragging the tow rope behind me. The water's not deep, but my legs are quickly soaked up to the knees. I bang my head on a horizontal metal girder and swear. From hereon in I swear to myself a lot. All the way in and pretty much all the way out. It's a bit like talking oneself up.

It must have been quite a feat lifting these heavy churns into place. It will have been dark and I can imagine the fevered activity and their nervousness, never quite sure if the Security Forces are going to turn up unannounced and *slot* them. Shame that, because if they had, it would have saved me all this sweat.

The silver grey churns stand close together linked with white Det Cord. Altogether there's six full-size churns and a half-size creamery can. Inside each churn will be the main HME charge and a booster charge. I look for electric detonator leads but can't see them. Logically it's going to be on the far side since that's where the Command Wire enters the tunnel. The whole thing is so big I can't easily get around it. Squeezing past and possibly disturbing a churn isn't a viable option for obvious reasons. My breath is rapid, shallow now. I feel light-headed and I'm still cursing. I'd like to say my mind is crystal clear but it isn't. My senses are straining for anything out of the ordinary. Outside, everyone is behind cover, nervously anticipating the outcome of my approach, waiting ... probably wondering what the bloody hell I'm doing that's taking so long. How many minutes have actually passed since I entered the tunnel, I do not know. But it feels as if I've taken too long. I abandon an attempt at getting to the detonator. Instead I get on with what I primarily set out to do. I thread the thick rope through the handles of two milk churns. Extracting two churns at a time will reduce the number of approaches I have to make. I don't cut the Det Cord because I can't be absolutely sure that it is Det Cord.

Sure enough I can see a face peering through a hedge. Without camouflage cream his bare skin almost glows in the dark hedge. This is quite disconcerting and everything comes to a grinding halt immediately.

I make my way out of the tunnel and climb back up the bank. Then I walk fairly casually back to the Control Point but watching the ground extremely carefully. Important in order to avoid stepping into a cow pat. Back at the Control Point, I pass the revised estimate of the device size to the Incident Commander and HQ Bessbrook.

Using our vehicle's four wheel drive capability we drag the first two churns out into the light of day. It's a bit of a battle. The vehicle skids around and the tow rope stretches alarmingly such that if it snapped it would probably take someone's head off. It doesn't, so the extraction is fairly uneventful. In all I have to make four approaches into the culvert. As they are extracted I line the churns up against the thick concrete retaining wall ready for the next phase.

Someone taps me on the shoulder. 'We're being watched,' he says, and points to a rise some 200 metres behind us. Sure enough I can see a face peering through a hedge. Without camouflage cream his bare skin almost glows in the dark hedge. This is quite disconcerting and everything comes to a grinding halt immediately. I notify the incident commander and we take cover. In the Cortreasla Bridge incident six years ago which wiped out the Bessbrook team, something similar to this occurred. A man was seen then but no action was taken. We've learned from that.

The radio traffic hots up and in short time the throbbing vibration of a helicopter engine is heard. It rears up into view over a hedge and skids to a halt in an adjacent field. As we watch, soldiers pour out of the machine and the guy is apprehended and bundled away.

We get back to work. Some time later we're informed that the face is a local farmhand whose curiosity has apparently got the better of him. Well fine, but I remain sceptical. The people who detonate these devices are just like him. They're local, know the area and appear very normal when you see them in court. In his case his curiosity could easily have got him killed because if something untoward had occurred at the time he was spotted, he would have taken the can for it. Soldiers are, for a number of historical reasons, very twitchy during these operations.

I recover the electric detonator still attached to a piece of Det Cord. A made-up test circuit and bulb is also found which the bomber has used to test the electrical continuity of the device, but then, as if by magic, it is lost in the post-clearance activities, never to be seen again. Rolls of coloured insulation tape are also recovered, which the bomber has used to connect up all the bomb components. The rolls have been abandoned by the terrorist because a court of law has undoubtedly educated them in the folly of retaining them.

The device is neutralised now but isn't completely rendered safe. Each churn could contain a secondary switch of some sort. Three ATOs have already died having underestimated the lethal potential of milk churns. The clearance continues therefore. Over the next hour or so I'm backward and forward setting and firing specialised cutting charges and when we run out of the charges, I up-end the remaining churns with ropes and shake out the contents. At the end of this exercise everything is spread about and visible and so I'm able to declare the thing safe.

Two types of home-made explosives have been used and I take 30g samples of each for forensic evidence. As the explosives are fertiliser-based, the bulk of it is spread out on the fields. This is standard procedure because they're quickly desensitised by moisture and soon absorbed into the ground. The second explosive type is the booster charge and this contains a chemical called nitrobenzene. NB has a very strong smell of marzipan. To try and contain this distinctive stink it is often wrapped in layers of polythene. NB is a compound that contaminates everything it comes into contact with. I wear plastic

50% of the way through the Operation. The churns have been extracted from the culvert; neutralised but yet to be rendered safe.

Most of the churns are cut in half, the others up-ended to spill out the contents.

gloves when handling it because it's corrosive, carcinogenic and easily absorbed through the pores of the skin. These attributes may or may not be understood by PIRA. If not then a lot of their operatives can expect to have serious health problems in due course.

I dissolve this explosive in copious amounts of water before spreading it out on the field in the same way. We clear down and pack up.

I still have the terrorist firing point to think about but with light fading fast, it's a job for tomorrow. I ask the troops to call in the chopper and we're extracted back to Bessbrook HQ. Not the infantry though. On this occasion they stay out on the ground to keep the area secure.

There's a good reason why we're extracted back to Bessbrook each evening. It's not, as is often unkindly suggested, because we aren't sufficiently hardy to withstand a night out on the freezing hills, but because we need to be on standby in the event of an emergency in Newry – or elsewhere for that matter. At least that's what I tell everybody.

5th February 1981

Booby trap, Chancellors Road, Bessbrook

Next day at first light I'm on the ground again. We set up the Control Point along the ridge line, about 100m from the terrorist firing point.

Wearing the IEDD suit this time and with both a Disrupter and hook and line, I make my way to the terrorist firing point. I step warily. The Royal Engineer Searchers have done their bit but the immediate area of the target is my concern. It's common for a pressure plate type device to be laid in these circumstances. On this occasion I'm very happy to find that the whole area has been recently trampled by cows.

Arriving at the firing point I see first the bright blue tape of the battery pack lying well exposed alongside the long wet grass and hedge. It comprises a set of large 9-volt batteries strapped together with blue adhesive tape. Looking to my left I see a gap in the hedge from where the terrorist bomber will have watched the traffic at the bottom of the hill. The culvert can be clearly seen. It's an ideal vantage point which must have been well reconnoitred by them beforehand. I

The Parachute Regiment search team is at work. The position of the firing cable has been drawn into the picture.

can imagine the bomber, CB radio in hand, nervously awaiting the tip-off from his compatriot parked at the entrance to the lane that the police car was on its way.

I lean forward to position the Disrupter and then catch my breath. I see a taut fishing line; very thin but unmistakable. It's attached to the battery pack. I lean forward. The other end disappears into the undergrowth.

Stepping to one side I carefully part the undergrowth and there, wrapped in a fertiliser sack, is a cast-iron gas cylinder which if full contains about 10lb HME. I take the whole thing in, in a second. The nylon fishing line is attached to the dowel pin of a plywood TPU. On this occasion it's providing the firing switch to the device via a pair of red and yellow electric detonator leads. The detonator is attached to a length of Det Cord protruding from the top of the cylinder.

I've seen enough and depart the scene to gather my thoughts.

Having talked it through with the team I return to the device sometime later. Attaching a hook and line to the plastic sack I pull the whole thing out of the undergrowth. Approaching it again I remove the detonator from the Det Cord and disconnect the leads from the

I lean forward to position the Disrupter and then catch my breath. I see a taut fishing line; very thin but unmistakable. It's attached to the battery pack. I lean forward. The other end disappears into the undergrowth.

The Victim Operated Device components with the Command Wire cable reel.

TPU. The whole thing is recovered intact. The battery pack gets X-rayed for good measure and the guts of it are found to be clear. We don't have equipment for opening up something as heavy duty as a cast-iron cylinder and unscrewing the metal bung is too risky. Therefore submitting it to the Forensic Science Laboratory is also too risky. I destroy it in a controlled explosion using 8oz of plastic explosives. Job done. Everything has gone pretty well – or so I think.

As we're packing up the SATO arrives. It's the first time I've seen him since our inaugural meeting. I'm polite and I try to relax but we're both ill at ease. He doesn't say anything to ease the situation and there are no words of praise for the team. The culvert device yesterday doesn't even get a mention. I wonder if he's actually disappointed. He sets to, fiddling with the forensic evidence and then the conversation is all about how I could have tackled the job differently. Normally I'd be happy to walk through the disposal approach but coming from him I'm unsure if it's legitimate criticism or pique because I've achieved something useful. It might sound unprofessional but that is how it was; a guy doesn't get on with his boss. How ordinary is that!

I don't argue with him. He has his say and leaves. Everyone else is elated though. It's been a great team effort and the infantry unit is well pleased. The CATO telephones me that evening and he's quite effusive. The photograph of the culvert device is displayed at the British Army Headquarters in Lisburn all the following week.

The PIRA planners have failed again and we can surmise that they're unlikely to let it ride. We hear a rumour that they are desperate for a success in our area. I guess their credibility depends on it; at least that's how they probably see it.

VIP visits

Periodically VIPs visit the Mill and I brief them on our work and also demonstrate Wheelbarrow. If we like them they get to play with it.

Anyone with an eye for detail will see in the top photograph that I have shielded this MP from a highly offensive but amusing poster that will get me into bother downstream. I am also showing off the latest technology for producing my IEDD Reports. And anyone with an eye for style will note that moustaches are de rigueur for soldiers wishing to exhibit that little *je ne sais quoi*!

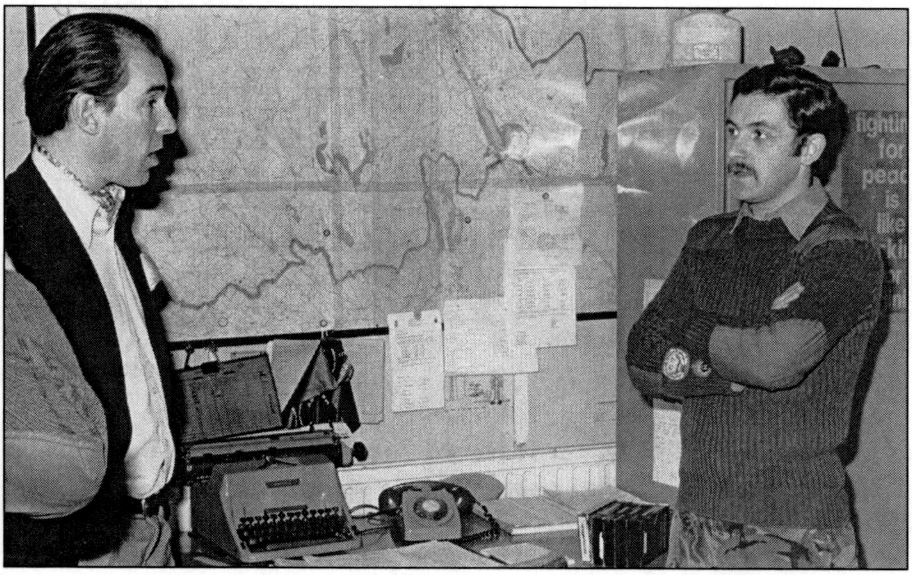

Discussing our role with a Member of Parliament.

The QLR Adjutant looks on as the MP demonstrates his prowess with our Wheelbarrow.

12th February 1981

Ambush Devices Border Crossing H25A

Eight months previously, on 14th June 1980, the Southern Irish police, the Garda, discovered a twin flex Command Wire on their side of the border near to the crossing we call H25A. The border at that place is delineated by a small stream and is not far from Crossmaglen.

The Garda cut the wire and threw the loose end into the North. From December 1980 a number of explosions have been heard in this area and on 25th January 1981 a farm owner reports damage to his adjacent outbuildings. A second Command Wire is then discovered by the Garda due south of the farm complex.

From our point of view this area 'stinks' and is therefore left to stew (or 'soak' as we tend to call it). The enemy is always trying to lure soldiers into a trap. They're very good at it but over the years we have also got a lot better at seeing through them.

The regiment decides to combine both clearances into one operation and on 18th February 1981 we go in. The Command Wire south of the farm is dealt with first. The Royal Engineers trace its whole length and measure it at 500 metres long. It's buried to a depth of 6–8 inches and has been in position for at least a number of years. It's a pig to remove and in the end we content ourselves with snapping it in lots of places and reburying the breaks, thereby rendering it unusable. The wire leads to a tight bend in a country lane. No device is discovered attached to it and so we move on to our next arranged Control Point to investigate the explosions and the second Command Wire.

This Command Wire straddles the border. It's been fed through a plastic hosepipe which is held in place on the bed of the stream by rocks. On our side it's well buried and difficult to trace but it points towards some dry stone walls that circle high ground overlooking the farm buildings, about 150 metres from the border. Displacing a couple of stones in the wall reveals a plastic fertiliser sack and inside is a stainless steel gas cylinder which I estimate to contains about 30lb of HME. A twig with an electrical detonator taped to it has been pushed into the explosives. The detonator is badly corroded having been in contact with the HME for quite some time. Corrosion can make detonators extremely sensitive. I remove it carefully. Using a hook and line the device is pulled out of its hiding place into the open and we go on to recover the remainder of the Command Wire. It's whilst we're reeling in the cable that a taped junction is spotted in the wire about 10ft from the device. This reveals a second twin flex cable. Stopping everything, everyone is evacuated from the immediate area

It's whilst we're reeling in the cable that a taped junction is spotted in the wire about 10ft from the device. This reveals a second twin flex cable. Stopping everything, everyone is evacuated from the immediate area to a place of safety again.

to a place of safety again. I come back and trace the twin flex cable to an adjacent wall just a few feet away from the first. Sure enough after tumbling the wall with a hook and line, I find a second gas cylinder hidden in the wall which is also wrapped in heavy plastic sheeting. This also has a corroded detonator pushed into the explosives which I carefully withdraw.

Whilst there's no firing mechanism to speak of, the danger is from the HME itself which has been mixed for some time and is potentially unstable. It could spontaneously combust and this would create either a low-order explosion or even burn to a high-order detonation. Either way it would be a shame to get myself killed at this late stage in the proceedings. Bringing water from the stream I do what I can to desensitise the explosives. Then I carry the cylinders into a field and destroy both in separate controlled explosions. We go on to investigate the derelict buildings. These have been destroyed by two relatively small explosions. It has taken two days to complete the operation.

The conclusions I draw are that the first Command Wire, laid some years previously, was to have been used in an attack on a Security Force patrol. The device would have been concealed behind the dry stone wall at a bend in the road where any vehicle would have had to

The Command Wire and position of the IEDs has been drawn into the picture.

The first device hidden in the dry stone wall at the end of the Command Wire.

The second device was wired to a junction in the Command Wire and designed to function simultaneously with the other.

slow down. Because green vehicles movements are banned now in this area the wire was to most intents and purposes redundant.

The explosions in the derelicts were completely separate. These were staged to entice SF into the area in order to utilise the two devices well concealed in the dry stone walls. Rusty food tins (ie army *compo*) were evidence that troops had at sometime in the not too distant past used the high ground as an Observation Post. Littering the countryside like this might eventually damage your mate's health!

24th February 1981

Car clearance, vicinity Omeath Road

Just over two months have passed since I arrived in the Province and I'm therefore halfway through my tour. Everything is going well thus far although we could do with more work. Boredom is one of our most despised enemies.

We're called out to deal with a suspect device in Woolworths. It turns out to be a hoax.

Later on I'm called to deal with a stolen car which has been dumped along a forestry track. It's been abandoned on the side of a steep hill and for good measure it's exposed to half of South Armagh. Since the reason why a car would be abandoned up here isn't clear, the risks are potentially many and the terrorist options varied.

Cars are used extensively by terrorists and clearing them is always problematic since there are many places in which explosives can be concealed. Each incident is unique and has its own idiosyncrasies. On the basis that any damage will write off the car, there's not much point going easy on them. That is unless there is a good reason to do so; like retaining forensic evidence.

On the basis that any damage will write off the car, there's not much point going easy on them. That is unless there is a good reason to do so; like retaining forensic evidence.

In the event I decide not to deal with the car out in the open. Instead I attach a tow rope to it and with our heli portable Land-Rover we drag it into tree cover. No mean feat as it doesn't entirely want to come in our direction and there is a danger of it plunging down the hill. In the event nothing untoward is discovered so the enigma of why it was abandoned miles from anywhere remains. Afterwards I wonder why I lay my life on the line to clear some crappy old car miles from anywhere which has already been written off by the insurance company. The answer is: because you're asked to.

Afterwards I wonder why I lay my life on the line to clear some crappy old car miles from anywhere which has already been written off by the insurance company. The answer is: because you're asked to.

Clearing a crappy old car. Why do we do it? Because we're asked to.

Having attached the rope to the car we're now going to pull the vehicle into cover.

28th February 1981

RPG-7 rocket attack, Dundalk Road, Crossmaglen

The austere, bland village of Crossmaglen is situated about 2km from the Border. It is staunchly Republican. At Partition, the populace couldn't believe it when they found that the border would pass to the south of the village and they would remain under British rule. PIRA hasn't let anyone forget this disappointment. It represents the great fault line to both sides. In military circles Crossmaglen has earned a bloody reputation all of its own.

The police station is now a military fortress. We have abbreviated its name to XMG. This is now an isolated post surrounded by hostile territory. It might not be politically correct to say that, but that's how it is. Everything is helicoptered in and out: policemen, cooks, contractors – even the rubbish. The station has been attacked on multiple occasions with just about everything PIRA could throw at it. There is a good deal in common with what service must have been like on the north-west frontier of India at the turn of the nineteenth century. The facilities are rudimentary to say the least. Some soldiers even live in freight containers. Others live in cramped, smelly squalor, crammed together in submarine bunks, ie three bunks high. Even so, morale is a lot higher than you might otherwise imagine. The lads don't do it for the money do they?

Soldiers patrol the streets and border area in multiples of 12 since smaller numbers are too easily overwhelmed. Armoured vehicles are used to provide support to them but there are no green vehicle movements outside of the immediate village.

I've heard a lot about Crossmaglen and I'm thinking of its grim reputation as my helicopter drops out of the sky like a brick into the police station yard below. The speedy rate of descent makes the machine a harder target for any aspiring sniper. At least that's what I hope.

Today I've been tasked to an RPG rocket and shooting attack on an army patrol. During the attack the Section Commander was shot in the chest with a high velocity round. Fortunately he was wearing a new type of flack jacket and this has saved his life. I don't take too much notice of this as I'm more concerned with getting out on the ground and investigating the explosive aspects of the incident.

I'm told that the rocket was fired at a Saracen armoured vehicle which had been supporting the foot patrol. It missed, passing overhead, and exploded some way beyond them. It might even have self destructed.

RPG-7

The Rocket Propelled Grenade (RPG-7) is used extensively in the Middle East but is now exported to trouble spots all over the world. No self-respecting group of radicals would be seen without an RPG launcher being shouldered by at least one of their number. This free flight rocket is highly inaccurate but utilising as it does the explosive 'shaped charge' effect it has a very effective penetrative capability should it strike a hard target. It will self destruct at about 1000m.

About to leave the police station, I stand behind a 10-ton Saracen armoured car looking at the large wriggly tin gates in front of me. My heart thumps as the gates are pulled back wide. The Saracen kicks into life and the soldiers who will accompany us fan out to the nearest cover quickly, making hard targets of themselves. With their monocular sights they then scan the streets, roof tops and windows and in this way they provide cover for the rest of us.

No one underestimates the dangers of walking out in this place, least of all yours truly!

The Saracen with its distinct whining engine noise lurches forward in a burst of blue exhaust fumes and I follow, leaving the relative safety of the fortress behind me. I walk alongside the vehicle as its .30 Browning machine gun swings from side to side and front to back as if daring anyone to get up to mischief. I look around me at windows and sky lights half open and my heart is somewhat in my mouth. This isn't something I would want to do too often. The vehicle protects me on one side but not the other. I could sit inside the vehicle but what would that look like! I grit my teeth and plod on. We don't meet many people. Those we do ignore us and they don't hang around; probably not wanting to get caught up in any potential crossfire.

I walk alongside the vehicle as its .30 Browning machine gun swings from side to side and front to back as if daring anyone to get up to mischief. I look around me at windows and sky lights half open and my heart is somewhat in my mouth.

I remember one Operator, a friend of mine, who had been awarded a medal for gallantry; when called out to support another team in Belfast took one look at the half open skylights and got straight back into the vehicle and waited there until he was required. When I saw this I realised afterwards that he was probably one of the bravest Operators I knew – or perhaps he was just sensible.

British soldiers walk these streets and lanes each and every day and every so often another dies. In one way it's Great Britain but in another it isn't anything like it.

We move along making good time; soldiers either side of the street move from doorways to gateways, from gateways to garden walls, keeping pace with the Saracen. It's serious stuff, scary. If a car had backfired I swear I would've had a heart attack! If we're ambushed I have to wonder what contribution I could make, armed as I am with only a 9mm pistol. The only advice I've been given on this so far is, 'Save the last one for yourself mate!'

We eventually arrive at the outskirts of the village and in the vicinity of the Telephone Exchange we carry out a search of the area. A nose and a tail section of a rocket are found in the vicinity of where it must have exploded. There's no evidence of any damage. Tracing back the likely flight path we try to find the launch point. This is usually easy to spot due to cardboard debris that's created on firing, but nothing is found. I make a sketch of the area and we then return to the police station the same way we came. I have to say it's a great relief when the gates close behind us.

I leave XMG for Bessbrook by the same Scout helicopter I arrived in. This chopper provides a taxi service between the two HQs. Because it's pretty much full, I elect to sit on the platform edge with my legs outside the helicopter, feet on the skids. The helicopter stokes up the revs and then lifts off like a rocket, gaining height as fast as possible for all the same reasons as when it arrived. In a couple of seconds we are at least a hundred or so feet above XMG.

Being perched on the platform, half in and half out of the chopper, was a good idea while the helicopter was on the ground, but as it lifts off I realise too late my mistake. The skids move out as the weight is taken off them and my backside leaves the platform. There's a loose webbing strap around me but it's only the pressure of my boot heels on the pole-shaped skid that is preventing me from dropping out of the helicopter. Panic wells up inside me as I try to get a hold onto the helicopter framework. I shout to the guy next to me to take hold of my jacket but I'm drowned out by the deafening noise of the engine. The helicopter then banks to the right and I'm overbalancing. Death is imminent. As the devil stares me in the face someone at last grabs my belt and pulls me back onto the platform. It's not the best but it'll do!

As I intimated earlier, I don't have a head for heights at the best of times so the journey back to Bessbrook is still a bloody nightmare. Nonetheless I arrive there at the same time as the helicopter. If people ask me how close I came to being killed in South Armagh, well this incident is right up there.

Under-car booby trap, Millvale Park, Bessbrook

Later that same day following my traumatic journey from XMG, I'm tasked to a small housing estate just a few hundred yards from Bessbrook Mill. I arrive at 21.40hrs and it's dark. In the dimly lit street I can see a row of white houses about 50 metres away. In front of one house is a Talbot Solara saloon car which has the driver's door half open.

The story is that the owner of the Solara is a Reserve Constable who is based at Bessbrook Police Station and the car is parked outside his house. About to get into his car earlier he glanced down and spotted a black box underneath the car. The way this is explained, or how I receive it at least, is that the box is on the ground below the driver's seat. This interpretation has unfortunate consequences for our RSP. In the dark and with high hedges opposite, I'm unable to get into a better position to confirm the exact location of the box and therefore I take it as read that it's on the ground.

Everyone has been evacuated from the adjacent houses so I decide to get on with the job. The Wheelbarrow is tooled up and whirrs off into the darkness towards the car. We peer into the mono TV monitor as it approaches the car. The half open door of the vehicle comes into view first. Despite some manoeuvring the door impedes our CCTV view of the car underside. I ask the No. 2 to push the door to, using the Wheelbarrow horizontal boom. He backs up the Wheelbarrow and then moves forward slowly. The boom is raised to the middle of the door and the Wheelbarrow inches slowly forward. Suddenly, 'Bang!'

Hard for me to understand how I didn't ascertain that the device was attached to the car.

There's a violent explosion, followed almost immediately by the sound of breaking glass and bits of metal clattering to the ground. Everyone leaps against the side of the Transit to shield themselves from the falling debris. Then silence.

What happened? Only now I discover that the box had in fact been attached to the car and wasn't on the ground at all. Bugger it! Had I realised this I would have had us tackle it in a completely different way. The type of device is now blindingly obvious. It's similar to that used to kill the politician Airey Neave in the Houses of Parliament car park. The box is clamped on to the car by powerful magnets. With a mercury tilt switch incorporated it is designed to function as the car moves off. It contains about 3lb of Semtex or a similar type of explosive. Moving the door had unfortunately rocked the car and this was sufficient to trip the tilt switch.

I apologise to the owner for our less than optimum performance. However he's much more concerned at the closeness of his escape and that of his family. It has also come as a great shock that he's been targeted by PIRA. The family will be relocated immediately. In due course they'll be compensated for the loss of their car.

At this exact moment, we're all pissed off that it got away from us. And I'm particularly galled that I didn't ascertain from my questioning exactly where the thing was located.

Police officers are especially vulnerable to this type of attack. They, and in fact everyone standing up for law and order, are barraged with personal security information to get them to check under their cars when they're left unattended. Too often people think it won't happen to them. He was lucky, but not everyone is.

At this exact moment, we're all pissed off that it got away from us. And I'm particularly galled that I didn't ascertain from my questioning exactly where the thing was located. The explosion has also damaged the Wheelbarrow. This is a shame because we recently refurbished it with camouflage paint and christened it 'Armageddon', – aptly it now seems. We don't christen any more Wheelbarrows after this. Superstitious? Not a bit of it.

The next day I get word that an Operator in Belfast, another Warrant Officer, has been chastised by the SATO for adapting his Wheelbarrow. We're all surprised by this because it has been this type of experiment and innovative thinking that has driven the improvements and modifications to our equipment. It's what got us through the multitude of different situations and scenarios. Not any more by the look of it.

Next day we take a run out to the 3 Brigade Headquarters at Portadown to replace the Wheelbarrow and replenish our explosives and ammunition. At lunch in the Sergeants' Mess I see a Staff Sergeant that I think I know from a previous life. This previous life was the three-year apprenticeship I attended in the 60s at the Army Apprentice College at Chepstow in Monmouthshire. I remember him as an Apprentice Corporal in a group a year senior to me. There was a pretty strict hierarchy at the College. The more senior groups ruled the more junior groups and there was a lot of 'fagging' and often bullying. I remember him as one of the nicer guys who didn't abuse the power he had. I approach him. 'Excuse me – weren't you at the Apprentice College at Chepstow around 1966? You were an electrician in B Company, Group 66C, I was Group 67B.' It is him and we exchange pleasantries about old times and how our military career paths have brought us to this point. He tells me he's based in Derry and travels around the Province in a civilianised vehicle servicing telecommunications equipment. We shake hands and wish each other well. I never expect to meet or hear of him again.

8th March 1981

Regiments turnover, ladies now present

The Queens Lancashire Regiment leave after handing over to the Royal Green Jackets. I'm introduced to the new people we'll be working with. From our perspective nothing much changes except in one key respect. The RGJ bring with them a troop of female soldiers from the Royal Signals who will 'man' the Telecommunications Centre. The girls are led by a Lieutenant of a similar gender.

Females have an impact on the workings of the HQ in a number of ways. One, it is a civilising influence, ie there are less naked men wandering about the place and the Anglo-Saxon gets toned down a bit. Two, the girls become the talk of the town for the chattering classes. Three, the tedious task of washing and drying clothes is now nightmarish. For example, everyone uses the same washing and drying machines. The protocol is that when a machine ends its cycle, the next person empties the contents onto the top of the machine so they can use it. The first time I come across a pile of ladies lingerie I find myself reacting like the stuff is red hot and I hastily beat a retreat. Am I, I wonder, the only one to struggle with this phenomenon?

Obviously not, because within a week or so I hear that all the women's underwear has been stolen. Not hard to imagine by whom. The situation is an emergency – for the girls anyway, who have to send out to Belfast for more. I hope they get compensated. After this I think they are given their own machines and the guys learn to get their kicks in other ways.

Whether anyone will admit to it or not, tension of a sexual nature now exists in the Mill. Caption competitions have been and remain common. These now take on a somewhat lurid note. The lady officer becomes the focus for all the alleged witticisms and via the Notice Board receives a barrage of very inappropriate comments, propositions and less than covert suggestions. To her credit she seems to take it all within her stride and treats all the unwarranted attention as a joke. Things begin to settle down as everyone gets more used to the new culture but the underlying pressure remains. Then one day it leaps into focus when I least expect it. I occasionally drop into the Ops room to see if there is any business brewing. Today all is quiet which I can tell from the minimal radio traffic. Only the Ops Sergeant appears present

Mixing men and women in operational circumstances isn't so common in 1981 but it's getting more so. How they'll all cope with the 'it' factor in future is beyond me!

and he's manning the radios. But from his faraway look and flushed demeanour I can see that something is bothering him; he appears distracted. As I get into the room fully I can see why. In fact I doubt that he would have heard the mortar alarm had it gone off. I can't fault him frankly because I become quickly distracted myself. It's the good lady Lieutenant, sitting opposite him passing the time of day and swinging her legs about. Having just played a game of squash by the look of it she is very fetching in her white kit. This may seem fairly innocuous to people back in Blighty where normality is normal, but not to red-blooded soldiers who are a long way from that place and have been for some time; if you catch my drift. A sentence immediately leaps into my mind that incorporates words like, 'very, eyes, sore and sight'.

Mixing men and women in operational circumstances isn't so common in 1981 but it's getting more so. How they'll all cope with the 'it' factor in future is beyond me!

Preventative action needs to be taken etc. Long bare legs and short white kit are all very well, but not now; not when we must remain focused on outwitting the enemy and responding quickly to mortar alarms. Someone has to do this and it doesn't look as if the

Sergeant is making any moves in that direction anytime soon. With a deep breath I ask her if she's got a minute and take her to one side. In a wholly patronising but quiet and kindly manner I whisper that she might want to tone it down a bit. I'll leave it to a psychologist to explain what the 'it' is. A little embarrassed and I expect more knowledgeable as to the complexities and weaknesses of men, she departs the room; sadly, only ever to be seen again in much more sensible clothing. Well, in the Ops room at least.

At a later date during a social call at my office, she gets one over me by drawing attention in a serious manner to the controversial poster on the cabinet that reads 'Fighting for peace is like F****** for virginity.'

Amusing as it is, I'm quite embarrassed that she, a female of the lady type should be exposed to such a profanity. 'I'm sorry Ma'am,' I mumble, somewhat colouring up. My No. 2 abandons me, raising his eyebrows as he goes. There's nowhere to go with this for the poster

Seeing my discomfort she can't keep a straight face and bursts out laughing; as does everyone else. The poster is safe. On operations it isn't just bombs, bullets and dead bodies. Sometimes it can even be a bit of a laugh.

represents the ATO Section's contemporary nonconformist and avant-garde view of army life. Seeing my discomfort she can't keep a straight face and bursts out laughing; as does everyone else. The poster is safe. On operations it isn't just bombs, bullets and dead bodies. Sometimes it can even be a bit of a laugh.

18th March 1981

Explosion, Louis Boyds Outfitters, Newry

I'm two-thirds through my tour so it's into the last straight. Over the previous fortnight I've been called to clear a tractor that a farmer was suspicious of, and on another occasion to destroy an IRA home-made mortar bomb which had been discovered in a field. Otherwise business has been slow.

My Royal Sigs ECM expert leaves us at the end of his tour of duty and we welcome his replacement, Kevin Meadows, onto the team.

At 21.00hrs on 18th March, two men are seen to hang a blast incendiary device onto the security grill of a men's outfitters in O'Hagen Street. Some 15 minutes later a warning is telephoned to the police station at Forkhill that a bomb has been left in Newry. The device explodes only five minutes after the warning is given. Fortunately SF reacted immediately after the men were spotted planting it and the area had been cleared. Otherwise there could easily have been serious casualties.

'Blue lighting' it to the incident and travelling at speed, we're ambushed by a group of youths gathered at a street corner. They hurl bricks at us as we pass them by. Before the protective metal grill can be pulled up my Transit windscreen is smashed. Fortunately the brick doesn't break through the windscreen.

We don't stop. By the time we arrive at the outfitters the fire has been extinguished and the Fire Brigade are all over the scene. The ground floor of the shop is gutted. There's nothing for me to do except pick up the fragments of device and write my report.

Next day I'm called to clear the car that was used in the attack and in a separate incident I'm flown to Forkhill after sparks are reported in a dry stone wall as a soldier climbed over it. Nothing untoward is found at either incident.

24th March 1981

Scania truck clearance, Forkhill

At 10am I get a call from the Ops room. I'm told they're tracking an incident and I may be needed. I place the team on standby. A large Scania truck carrying at least 20 tons of grain had been hijacked the night before. In the events that followed the hijacking, a mechanic from Forkhill was shot in the neck and subsequently died of his wounds in a hospital in Dundalk. Should the truck reappear I will have to clear it.

I speak with the Police Liaison Officers and the following is what is alleged to have happened: the truck was being used to smuggle grain across the border. When it doesn't arrive at its destination by the due time, the truck owner assumes it has broken down. He drives to Forkhill and picks up his mechanic. From there the pair back-track the pre-arranged route the truck should have taken. They come across the truck in a narrow country lane but as they approach a gunman steps out of the shadows and indicates that they are to stop. Instead, the owner puts his foot down and drives at the gunman who leaps out of the way. The car scrapes down the side of the truck and careers off down the lane. At which point a gunman opens fire on them. The car gets through but with the driver shot in the hand. The mechanic is hit in the neck. The car doesn't stop but is driven straight to the hospital in Dundalk.

Meanwhile, the original truck driver is being held hostage in an adjacent field. He's now given a car and told to clear off. Unbeknown to PIRA he's an ex-member of the Ulster Defence Regiment so he's a very lucky man. In the rear view mirror he sees the truck headlights come on as the truck is started up.

The first anyone at Bessbrook learns of the truck's whereabouts is when the incident is reported on the lunchtime television news. A journalist is giving his report and being filmed next to the truck which is now parked in a lane near Cortreasla Bridge. The truck seems to have incurred a flat tyre.

An operation is mounted to recover the truck.

Clearing a 30-ton truck so that it can be declared safe ain't easy; there's scope to hide all sorts of things. It's critical therefore to get a thorough understanding of exactly what transpired on that fateful night since this will give me a better understanding of the risks I'm faced with.

Smuggling

I'm reliably informed that smuggling is prevalent across the international border. It seems to be a way of life here. With the police restricted in what they can control and customs posts regularly targeted by PIRA, the previous decade has been a bonanza for those so inclined. I surmise that this is one of the main motivations for keeping the conflict going longer than is politically necessary.

We piece the incident together and this is how I come to understand it. The grain was being smuggled across the border via an unapproved crossing. Somehow the local warlord got wind of it and not having agreed to the consignment passing through his territory he had it intercepted. It's likely that the gunmen were waiting for the truck owner to turn up. I think that the hijackers were blinded by the car headlights and didn't know who it was in the car that failed to stop and they shot blindly at it in a fit of pique. With the area compromised they moved the truck to its current location and let its tyre down, still expecting the owner to turn up. When he didn't appear by daylight they melted away.

This scenario has the ring of truth about it. If so, it was unlikely that much time had been spent by the hijackers preparing anything particularly nasty.

We mount the CCTV camera high and I search the truck the best I can using the Wheelbarrow. Wearing the IEDD suit I clear the cab and engine compartment. A driver is eventually sent for to move the truck and I have to persuade him it is safe to do so. To give him confidence I take off the suit and get him to start it up with me standing next to him. I walk alongside as he pulls away. He breathes a sigh of relief when nothing happens. Me too.

We would have towed a much smaller vehicle away from the scene but this is too big. I have to get on with it. Such an RSP might not have got me through the NI Pre-Ops course for in theory there is much that could have gone wrong, but if you try and think of every single scenario the terrorist could cook up you would quickly go mad. Certainly nothing would get done. The alternative is to destroy every vehicle you're tasked to, just to be safe. As I say, it's important to try and ascertain what the other guys are trying to achieve.

Getting dressed is a two-man task

To give him confidence I take off the suit and get him to start it up with me standing next to him. I walk alongside as he pulls away. He breathes a sigh of relief when nothing happens. Me too.

LCpl Meadows, our new 'Bleep', zips me into the suit.

1st April 1981

A little local pressure?

Following an intelligence tip-off that there is a bomb in the area, Royal Engineer Search teams are tasked to clear a lane near Clontigora. They discover Det Cord and strips of insulating tape in the road alongside a dry stone wall. No device. The story is that the locals became unhappy with an ambush bomb that had lain in this position for sometime and they were concerned that it might have become unstable. PIRA were informed and removed it for them! I wonder? Not an April fool, surely?

In the evening I read a report that two soldiers have been shot and killed, ambushed on their way to repair a telecommunications mast in the Derry area. One of them is the guy I met at Portadown from the Apprentice College at Chepstow. Not just a name on the page this time; not just another statistic. This time I see the face and hear the voice and I feel the wretchedness of his family deep inside me.

Not just a name on the page this time; not just another statistic. This time I see the face and hear the voice and I feel the wretchedness of his family deep inside me.

2nd April 1981

Under-car explosion

Next day at midnight I'm called to the Ops room and notified that an explosion involving a car has occurred in a country lane north of Newry. Green vehicle movements are not banned in that direction and so I decide to travel to the incident via our Transit vehicles.

It's cold, dark, damp and foggy when we set out. Visibility is minimal. We make slow progress. Twenty minutes later we're in the country lane and approaching the rendezvous (RV). Then in the headlights we see the white tape strung across the road. We drive up to it and I dismount and look around. It's deathly quiet and very eerie. I notify Bessbrook that we're at the scene but that no one is present to meet us. Bessbrook confirms that the police are on the ground so I assume the Incident Commander is at the other end of the lane. Taking a torch I step over the white tape and make my way down the road. It's a 'pea souper' and I'm straining to see into the darkness. Walking down the centre of the road looking forward I suddenly stumble and realise I've put my foot in a shallow hole. Pointing the torch down I see immediately that it is in fact a shallow crater; the seat of an explosion. To the left is a brick wall of a garden which is peppered and chipped from shrapnel strikes. All around me I can now see small bits of metal and debris. I walk on. Within a few paces I have to step over identifiable male body parts lying in the road. Then I come across the burnt-out almost unrecognisable rear section of a car.

All around me I can now see small bits of metal and debris. I walk on. Within a few paces I have to step over identifiable male body parts lying in the road. Then I come across the burnt-out almost unrecognisable rear section of a car.

Seconds later I hear voices and streams of torchlight cut through the mist further down the lane and a number of police officers appear out of the gloom. I introduce myself and the senior police officer explains what he knows. 'It's a bad business this,' he says, but I've already deduced that much. At about 23.00hrs a civilian living in the house adjacent to the crater reported an explosion in the road outside. When the agencies arrive they discover that a Ford Fiesta has blown up and caught fire. The driver is still alive and it turns out he is an RUC Constable stationed at Bessbrook Police Station (this is a different

A Policeman's life cut short. Another family decimated.

establishment to Bessbrook Mill). On completing his duty the Constable had collected his car from the nearby housing estate and driven home. He routinely parked in the housing estate because Bessbrook Police Station doesn't have its own car park! This is a shock to me for the risk to Police Officers working at that establishment is so blindingly obvious.

Because he was conscious when taken away in the ambulance, the Senior Police officer is optimistic about the policeman's chances. But from what I have seen in the road, I am fairly certain he isn't going to make it and to reduce his expectations I say so. Sadly the guy died en route to the hospital.

Piecing this incident together I conclude that the device was fitted to the car shortly before the Constable arrived at it. This type of device has a timer incorporated which provides the bomber with a delay before it arms. The timer was therefore in all likelihood still running when the Constable got into the car. Some ten minutes later the device armed and the car's movements simultaneously triggered the firing circuit. Travelling at speed, probably before the mist came down, the car broke up and burst into flames.

This device would have been similar to the one we dealt with four weeks previously. Tragically, the Constable had not checked under his car and this cost him his life.

15th April 1981

Blast incendiary, Norbrook Laboratories

Business is slow. In the previous period I've only had to deal with a couple of incidents that both turned out to be false alarms. They prevented us from getting too bored at least. Then at midnight on 15th April an explosion is reported at the Norbrook Pharmaceutical Laboratory in Newry. The explosion has gutted the first floor of the building. A further device is reported by the owner. It's been placed in a 'Sterilisation Room' and from its description it's a blast incendiary.

At the Laboratory I find that the Wheelbarrow can't be used because there are too many doors to negotiate and these would trap the umbilical cord. A manual approach is therefore necessary. I get dressed in the IEDD suit and my No. 2 primes a Disrupter and fits it into its purpose-built stand.

Armed also with a sketch of the room and floor layout I walk into the building and through the final door. There it is staring at me. To all intents and purposes it's exactly the same as the device at the Killeavy truck yard; albeit the dowel pin isn't present this time. The can has all the same possibilities.

I place the Disrupter muzzle within an inch or two of the TPU and leave the room. The Disrupter will pretty much disintegrate the wooden box but unfortunately there's nothing in my armoury that is less powerful. If I use some other technique or try to be innovative I'll be right in the shit from you know who if it goes wrong. Despite the low probability of anything going wrong, I can't risk it.

Bang! the Disrupter is fired. I give it a few minutes and re-enter the room. The TPU and the can are both smashed and it takes only a second or so to make sure all the bits of device remaining are completely separated out. Satisfied that the device is safe I go to collect the Disrupter but find that it's missing from the stand – there's no sign of it. I'm puzzled and I look around the floor but sure enough it's gone. I take off my helmet and then I see that the electrical firing cable is hanging from the ceiling next to the entrance. The Disrupter has recoiled out of the stand and penetrated right through the ceiling.

I pull on the cable to recover the Disrupter. I should have been wearing the helmet because half the bloody ceiling plaster comes crashing down onto my head. Brilliant! When I come out of the building I look like Mr Pastry!

I pull on the cable to recover the Disrupter. I should have been wearing the helmet because half the bloody ceiling plaster comes crashing down onto my head.

18th April 1981

Kidnapping, Jonesborough

On 18th April we're flown to Jonesborough; a town that straddles the border on the east of our area. A farm labourer is reported to have been kidnapped by armed men, probably PIRA. His car has since been spotted in the town. It's located within a few metres of the border. We need to be clear about where the border is for obvious reasons and I'm amazed to find that it passes through the middle of an adjacent farmyard. There's nothing on the ground to distinguish the border at all.

Highly porous is one way of describing it. But to me it exists merely to constrain the activities of the security authorities on both sides of the fence. The RUC do liaise with the Garda fortunately and the latter are in evidence on their side of the border throughout the operation. But because we aren't allowed over the border, the Royal Engineer Searchers have to pass within 25 metres of the car in their search for buried Command Wires. This is not ideal.

The two police forces seem to be quite relaxed with each other but it is less than politically correct for the Garda to liaise directly with the British Army.

Using the shotgun fitted to the Wheelbarrow we open up the car bonnet and then the boot. I half expect to find either a body or a bomb, but in the event there's neither. I don the IEDD suit and approach the car. Judging by the amount of straw and farmyard debris present the owner must have kept pigs or cattle in it. A jacket lies on the back seat and I check it out. I'm amazed to find that the pockets are stuffed with wads of money – Irish punts. How he came by that amount of money I do not know. Perhaps it's a clue to what's happened to the owner.

In South Armagh, PIRA apparently see themselves as public protectors when it suits them. The money might therefore be the profit from some nefarious activity that has come to their attention. Anyway I can only surmise. I pass it all to the RUC for safe keeping.

A couple of days later I hear that the lad has been set free by his kidnappers having been given, I guess, the fright of his life.

Half the farm buildings are in the South, half are in the North. The suspect car can be seen on the right.

19th April 1981

Attack on Warrenpoint Police Station

It's the following day and late evening when I'm called to the Ops room for a task briefing. I'm told that a van parked opposite the police station at Warrenpoint has roused police suspicions. The RUC are carrying out more checks but it looks serious. We are to move out at 2am under additional escort. In the meantime we should get some rest as it's going to be a long night. I try to get some sleep but it's impossible.

We move out on time. In order to avoid the possibility of ambush we take a circuitous route to the town of Warrenpoint.

As the convoy rolls into Warrenpoint it's cold and misty and the streets are empty and silent. At the corner of the main street we're met by a police officer who is our contact. Together we peer around the corner and he points out the police station about 100 metres away. Its frontage is illuminated by a variety of bright security lights. Around the building are the concrete blocks linked by steel poles which are used everywhere to prevent car bombs from being placed too close to buildings, thereby limiting the structural damage they can cause. The police officer points out the suspicious Ford Escort van which is easy to see, parked as it is all alone on the opposite side of the wide street.

The police officer brings me up to speed on the story so far. A farmer known to the police always parks his van in that spot on market days. Nothing suspicious there. However, when the vehicle was

It's cold and quiet and the van opposite the police station has been 'twinned'. I take aim at the rear windows with the shotgun and I'm probably much too close.

still there at 10pm the police telephoned the owner at his home to ask why he hadn't taken it away. The farmer replied that his van was in actual fact parked out the front of his house. A police patrol was quickly diverted to the farm and sure enough what the farmer had said was confirmed. The van at the police station was therefore bogus. It had been 'twinned', ie re-sprayed and fitted with a number plate the same as the farmer's.

What then followed was either heroic or foolish, others can decide. Before my arrival the police allowed a constable to conduct a rather alarming and risky reconnoitre of the van. Putting on a civilian jacket and waving an empty beer bottle, he staggered and swayed his way up the main street pretending to be a drunk. Arriving at the van he rolls onto the bonnet and then having peered inside, continues to amble on up the road until he is far enough away to be safe. The constable is now able to inform me that, 'The van's empty except for a narrow roll of old carpet across the back doors'.

If PIRA's intention is to attack the police station then an empty van doesn't stack up. But the police station isn't the only potential target. PIRA have clearly gone to a lot of trouble to arrange this and there are a variety of places where a device can be hidden in a van. An anti-handling switch is an obvious option but there could still be a timer running down on us. Both are easily feasible. Another likely option is that the device is radio controlled (RC). If so we can be certain that the terrorist is watching the scene even now from a vantage point somewhere in the vicinity. If it is RC the bomber might fire the device if he suspects we've sussed his plan. As we're some distance away and around the corner we might assume he doesn't know we're on to him just yet.

After a quick discussion with my Royal Sigs ECM expert, we conclude that the best way of dealing with this is to drive the ECM Transit vehicle forward with the ECM equipment transmitting 'white noise'. This is called the direct approach. The electronic field we transmit can be expected to confuse a radio control receiver. The hope is that the bomber, seeing us approaching, might initially think we're driving into his killing zone. When we're about 50 or so metres from the suspicious van we'll swing the vehicle across the road and this will become the IEDD Control Point. Troops will pan out and secure the area. Even if the bomber realises then that we're on to him and tries to transmit a firing signal, the radio control receiver by then won't be able to pick out the firing signal. Any such device will therefore be under our control. That's the plan anyway.

The police and troops are briefed. The ECM equipment is switched on and we take a break as it has to warm up. Suddenly there's a muffled 'thump', a sound like a low velocity gun shot. Somebody speaks for all of us: 'What the f*** was that?' For a second there's confusion and everyone goes to cover. A policeman appears and tells me he thinks the sound came from the van. I peer around the corner of the building and using the binoculars study the van. There's no sign that anything has changed. No smoke, broken glass or anything untoward. I have my suspicions but not enough to change the plan.

The police and troops are briefed. The ECM equipment is switched on and we take a break as it has to warm up. Suddenly there's a muffled 'thump', a sound like a low velocity gun shot.

We move off with me walking alongside the front vehicle. We're quite exposed in the middle of the street and there's no additional security at this point so it's a little unnerving to think we're possibly being watched by PIRA from a skylight or window. Approximately 50m from the van I tell the driver to swing the vehicle across the street. At this point, troops from either end of the street appear and seal it off. The suspect van is now well within the range of our ECM equipment, so hopefully we are in control of any RC switch.

There are no houses within the immediate vicinity so no one to evacuate. With the area now secured by the SF we can get on with the clearance. I take our Browning shotgun and shoot out the rear windows of the van. Using the RCV Wheelbarrow we manoeuvre into position a 2oz explosive charge inside and to the centre of the vehicle.

The small explosive charge rang out in the empty street and the photographer clearly jumped out of his skin.

After giving a warning, the charge is fired and the sharp bang echoes up and down the empty streets. The violent over-pressure completely detaches the van roof and throws open the rear doors – perfectos! The explosion wakes up the whole town and also the fire alarm in the fire station at the other end of the street. It's a hell of a din. Retained firemen suddenly appear from a variety of doors pulling jackets over pyjamas and we watch as they rush in to report for duty.

With the smoke cleared we move in again with the Wheelbarrow CCTV. We pan the camera left and right. In the grainy mono picture we can see a spare tyre and some tools but there's little else to raise our suspicions. Using the binoculars I can make out the roll of carpet hanging half in and half out of the rear doors but the situation remains unsettling and is far too ambiguous for my liking. There's nothing for it however but to approach the van and eyeball it.

As I get ready to approach the van the questions in my head are: Where did that earlier explosion arise from? Has a timer expired and fired a detonator or could our ECM equipment have inadvertently initiated something? Has the terrorist tried to initiate it but failed?

With a torch I walk up to the rear of the van and peer in. I see the back of both driver and passenger seats. There's nothing suspicious in the cargo area. It's empty like the constable said but pointing the torch down I see something familiar which was missed with the CCTV; it's whitish, 'Bloody hell, Det Cord!' A length of it runs from between the front seats along the floor of the van towards me. I look down at the roll of carpet next to my leg and my heart skips a few beats ... 'Jesus Christ, it's the f*****g bomb!' Yes there is an old rug, but it's wrapped around a metal gas cylinder which is looking an awful lot bigger than it did when it was purely a rug ten or so minutes ago. It's quite a shock! When my heart starts up again it's pounding like a good 'n.

With a torch I walk up to the rear of the van and peer in. I see the back of both driver and passenger seats. There's nothing suspicious in the cargo area. It's empty like the constable said but pointing the torch down I see something familiar which was missed with the CCTV; it's whitish, 'Bloody hell, Det Cord!'

I gather my thoughts and contemplate whether discretion would indeed pass for the better part of valour. I decide to tough it out. Walking to the front of the vehicle I shine the torch into the passenger well. There is the electronic switching arrangement contained in an open Tupperware box. I can also see the remains of detonator leads. The detonator has indeed fired but this hasn't propagated to the 40lb of high explosives in the gas cylinder and it isn't hard to see why.

The 'small' gas cylinder lies in the street behind the shattered van after IEDD action.

The proximity of the van to the fortified police station can be seen here.

The van after the clearance.

Wicks and I empty the explosives from the cylinder.

The 40lb of explosives would have made a mess of anyone in the vicinity of the police station.

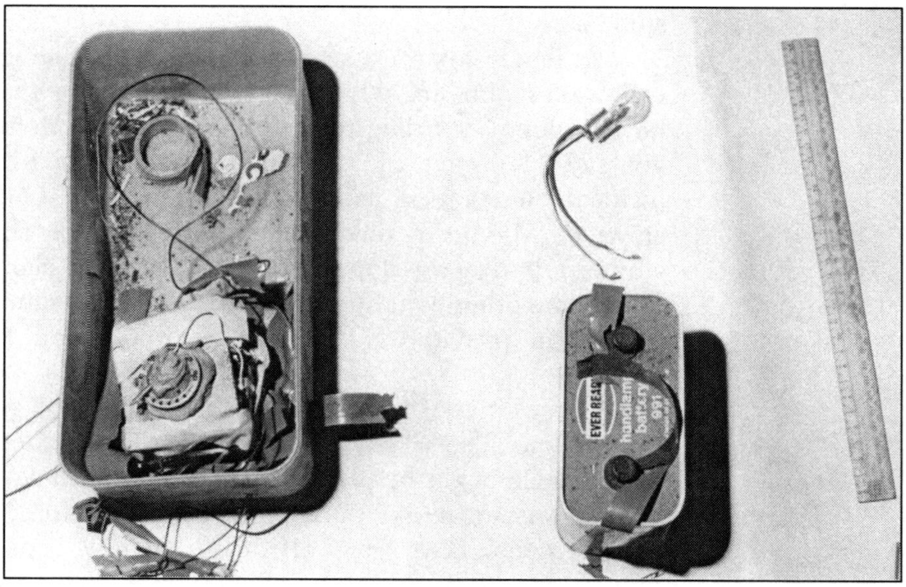

The radio control switch and battery recovered with the Tupperware container.

The Det Cord is comprised of bits, taped together to make a long length. The end is shattered where it has failed to pick up the blast wave when the detonator functioned. All the elaborate planning that PIRA must have put into this attack has been let down by poor quality explosives.

The switch is contained in a Tupperware box with a large blue battery and is indeed radio controlled. Our operating instructions oblige me to notify CATO or SATO of any incident involving radio controlled switches, so I try. Unfortunately I can't use my PYE radio because we're out of range of HQ Bessbrook. Instead I ask the Incident Commander if he would kindly notify Bessbrook with his more powerful radio and relay a message to my bosses for me. I naively think it will get through.

Dawn is breaking as we clear up and bag the forensic evidence. Everyone is weary now and there is nothing to be gained from hanging around Warrenpoint town centre as the town wakes up. I decide to take the team back to Bessbrook. Given the circumstances I think that everything has gone OK, except that I realise now that I'm too susceptible to 'autosuggestion'. When someone tells me something and there's no reason to believe otherwise, I accept it at face value. This 'phenomenon' also occurred at the under-car booby trap at Millvale Park.

You do your best. You think you have a handle on it but there is this great potential to be caught out. Most survive these aberrations; some die.

At Bessbrook there's no sign of the SATO, so I telephone him. The call wakes him up, which is the first inkling that communications haven't gone according to plan. 'Did you get the message I relayed to you sir?' He hasn't. He asks what it's all about. I begin to explain the incident but as soon as he hears the words 'RC device' he becomes enraged. My heart sinks. He yells down the phone, calling me a women's body part. He offers me no further chance to explain and after some other equally flowery expletives he slams the phone down. It's a real pity the call wasn't recorded, you know, for training purposes.

I brace myself for the storm to come and he gets to Bessbrook in record time. The wheels must have hardly touched the tarmac. Now most people might be pleased the job had been completed safely. Not him, he has a face like thunder. If it wasn't before, I can see it's definitely personal now. He's affronted, mainly because an RC device should have been his shout; passed to him. He wants to speak with me alone. Finding an empty office he begins what quickly becomes an interrogation. He states that I've deliberately disobeyed Standing Orders by not calling him out earlier. He begins to tear me apart. He doesn't shout but his words are like vitriol. He's driving in nails. He isn't interested in the complexity or the ambiguous nature of the task. He doesn't like the approach I took, the type of explosive weapon I used, the point that we switched on the Electronic Counter Measures. Nothing I say makes any sense to him. He broadens his attack into my general abilities as a Warrant Officer, which, if true, should have been raised before now. He talks about sacking me. For 45 minutes I have to endure this crap, this petulance. In the army you can't walk with your feet, you have to bear it; even if you're having trouble with the grin.

Any residual respect I might have had for the guy evaporated that night. With no sleep, I'm exhausted. The adrenalin has long since worn off. I'm struggling to take most of it in. I feel the black dog of depression barking. Finally he's finished, ending with a swan song around, 'I should have you replaced.' Having been forewarned at the beginning of the tour hadn't helped me to prepare for this.

Later he takes hold of the forensic evidence and begins to pull it apart, as he did at the Chancellors Road incident. From across the room I watch him remove components to examine them. Also watching this, the RUC Border Superintendent takes me to one side and tells me the SATO has probably ruined the forensic evidence. It's now inadmissible in court. But he's talking to the wrong guy. I tell him I'm not best placed to deal with it. I ask the Super to speak to him himself. Whether he does or not, I don't know. To be honest I'm beyond caring. I feel physically sick.

My difficult relationship with the SATO has finally erupted. At the team room it's hard to hide that I'm gutted. Initially they're confused but then begin to question whether what we are doing is safe. They question me. Who can blame them since decisions I make could obviously have consequences for them. They're also concerned as to whether they might be implicated in any fallout. Both times they've seen the SATO he hasn't had a good word to say to them. This matter has become a complete distraction which has more in keeping with what you might have expected in the Crimean War than a modern army. But in reality all life exists here as it does in any other walk of life.

After a couple of days mulling it over, I can't put the issue out of my head. The matter is eating away at me. I'm depressed – or in the army vernacular, 'seriously pissed off'. The team remains twitchy and uncertainty reigns supreme. I decide to take the matter to the only other person I could realistically take it to: the CATO.

I telephone HQ 321 at Lisburn. Unfortunately the CATO isn't in and so I'm put through to – guess who? I'm on the spot now.

He wants to know why I've asked to see the CATO. I tell him that given everything he's said to me, I feel I'm entitled to speak with the 'Commanding Officer' (sic). Of course my mistake is like a red rag to a bull. His reaction is pretty predictable. He says I'm more f****** stupid than he originally thought etc, etc. I begin to wonder if he's actually lost the plot. I don't even know if my request to see the CATO is passed through.

Three weeks pass following the Warrenpoint RC task. The team and I soldier on. I'm fed up, bad tempered and touchy and this has its negative impact on the team. The situation is crap, but then a soldier's life often is.

All goes quiet on the Bessbrook front. PIRA are probably taking stock of their failures and organising the next big thing. The hunger strikes at Long Kesh prison are drawing to their inevitable conclusion and PIRA won't want to draw attention away from this. Finally on 5th May Bobby Sands dies after a hunger strike lasting 66 days. There's rioting elsewhere in the Province but despite us anticipating it, his death doesn't bring us any immediate business. It's just a matter of time however.

Three weeks pass following the Warrenpoint RC task. The team and I soldier on. I'm fed up, bad tempered and touchy and this has its negative impact on the team. The situation is crap, but then a soldier's life often is.

8th May 1981

'Contact' on the border

Over the intervening period I deal with two minor incidents which turn out to be false alarms.

On 8th May I'm tasked to attend a 'follow-up' to an incident which has occurred on the border and has involved the COP. The story is that when the incident occurred the platoon was asleep in their daytime hide having been out on the ground the night previously. Their bored sentry crawled forward to a rise and to his amazement came across four armed and masked men moving away from him in file along the border. The distance was less than 50 metres. Scurrying back and waking the rest of the group he returned in time to open up on them as they disappeared into 'dead' ground. The fire fight which resulted went on for some considerable time and much ammunition was expended. Eventually one terrorist trying to make his escape found himself trapped in the corner of a dry stone wall on the other side of the border. The COP machine gunner tried his best to demolish the wall but no luck and the guy was fortunate enough to be arrested by the Garda before the wall completely collapsed. Another guy was discovered cowering in a ditch on our side of the border and was taken into custody. Found to be lying on a very nice Heckler Koch automatic rifle, he's lucky he wasn't shot. So if there is a shoot to kill policy in force in the Province – you know, like PIRA's – well someone should have told our boys. Two baddies managed to escape.

I make safe the abandoned weapons and bomb components they'd been carrying. Whatever it was they had planned to carry out it had been well thwarted. Incidents like this are good for the troops' morale.

Later that day I'm called to clear a car that the Garda believe was driven by the PIRA unit involved in the contact. They think it might be booby trapped. It isn't.

The border area where a PIRA unit was intercepted by the Close Observation Platoon. The ensuing firefight went on across the border for quite some time before two of them were finally arrested and taken into custody.

Mortar attack, Newtownhamilton

The 8th has already been a busy day when at 20.30hrs an infantry officer bursts through the office door and exclaims, 'Felix, can you come to the Ops room now, NTH is under attack.' He's excited and this is always contagious.

PIRA home-made mortar bombs

The mortar bombs currently in use by PIRA are large steel cylinders with fins, each of which contains up to 40lb of HME. The bomb has a range of a couple of hundred yards. PIRA use this weapon because it isn't constrained by standard fortifications. It provides them with a means of lobbing explosives over the highest walls.

'NTH' is the abbreviation for the military barracks and combined police station at Newtownhamilton. An infantry platoon are located there and cover the far west of our tactical area.

As we approach the Ops room I ask the officer when the attack happened.

'It's still happening,' he says.

'Bloody hell' I reply.

The burst of adrenalin can almost make you dizzy!

We enter the Ops room. The RGJ Commanding Officer is present and the radio traffic is hot. He says, 'Newtownhamilton has been mortared Felix. There are casualties. I'm going up there now. Hopefully the area will have been secured by the time we get there. Do you want a lift?' I reply that I would. He adds, 'Are you ready? We're leaving now.'

I race back to my office to collect my pistol and flack jacket. Just enough time to brief the team. I finish with, 'Follow me up in the vehicles. I'll meet you there.' Then I'm off.

Sometimes you don't have much time to think, planning is rudimentary. Your responses or choices are limited despite what may be suggested on the NI Pre-Ops IEDD course. In the real world, you make decisions as the incident unfolds around you. Paramount is providing everyone with confidence that you are the person to deal with it.

As we approach NTH the Gazelle helicopter drops down through the clouds. There's no sign of a fire, no smoke. The helicopter bumps down into the playing fields across the road from the base and we pile out. It immediately lifts off. Too much of a target to hang around.

Two soldiers appear from the side of a building. One of them is an Officer: the other with a rifle is his escort. The Officer greets the CO. We're told to move quickly – the area isn't yet secure. I follow them and we scurry across the main road into the relative safety of the barracks. Once behind the blasted wriggly tin walls I can see that an accommodation block is very badly damaged. The air is still thick, almost toxic with dust and the tell-tale smell of blasted HME. A

Sometimes you don't have much time to think, planning is rudimentary. Your responses or choices are limited despite what may be suggested on the NI Pre-Ops IEDD course. In the real world, you make decisions as the incident unfolds around you.

The SF accommodation block destroyed by PIRA mortar bombs

soldier passes us piggy backing another who has a bandage around his head and looks semiconscious. Another holding a rifle is wearing carpet slippers, no flack jacket. Clearly he's had to get out in a hurry.

We press on to the Ops room where the staff explain what has occurred so far. A Tipper lorry was being watched via the CCTV as it approached along the main road that passes by the base. Nothing odd with that, but then it stopped 100 metres away. At which point the driver was seen to dismount and disappear across the street. Almost immediately a small explosion was heard and the first mortar bomb was projected into the sky. This took with it the black polythene tarpaulin that had disguised the lorry contents from the air. Accordingly the bomb fell short and exploded in the street. Then, salvos of mortar bombs were seen on the CCTV erupting from the vehicle and hurtling towards them, smoke streaming from their tails. Most landed within the barracks but one overshot and hit a house.

Soldiers who were quickly deployed to secure the helicopter landing area were then fired on from the far side of the playing fields. One of the soldiers had a close escape. He shows me a bullet lodged in the heel of his boot.

Most of the bombs have hit and demolished the soldiers' accommodation block, which by an act of God was mainly empty at the time. The accuracy of the attack has been uncanny. Amazingly, the Security Forces haven't suffered any fatalities, albeit casualties are still being tended to. One shocked soldier, still hyper, recounts to me how he dived to the floor of his room when he heard the first explosion, at which point a mortar bomb crashed through the roof and embedded itself in the floor in front of him. He describes the tail fins to me. With just enough time to lift himself up and throw himself out of the room the bomb exploded. He found himself on the ground floor, dazed but unhurt. Fortunately for him this type of mortar bomb has a timer rather than an impact fuze. Twenty minutes after the first mortar left the truck a separate explosion occurred in the truck cab and demolished it.

I look into the grainy mono screen of the Ops room CCTV monitor; the truck is clearly visible. When I messed up the mortar job at the NI Pre-Ops course, I had it drilled into me that I must quickly ascertain the status of the firing platform. The big question is, have all the mortars fired? People are out in the open and a further salvo of mortars could have catastrophic consequences. I need to check this out, and quick, so I need to see into the truck.

Because the area is still not fully secure I'm provided with an armed escort. The two of us make our way to the main road. I have no equipment with me. I climb onto a garage roof nearby but I still can't see into the high-sided truck. There's nothing else for it but to get onto the truck itself. Now this puts me in a dilemma. Operating procedures state that a set time should elapse before a manual approach is attempted in case of secondary devices. That duration has not yet passed. The alternative is to escalate the matter to SATO/CATO for permission to approach the target within the time period. Well at the moment I'm standing on a garage roof without any communications.

The truck abandoned in the main street.

There's no time to make the call. No time to wait. I haven't time to explain the ins and outs to SATO. But I hesitate because this could be the man's chance to get shot of me. Should I cover myself? Should I return to the Ops room and refer the matter up? What if I appear in a newspaper photograph? For the first time in the tour I'm indecisive, I'm struggling. I'm thinking about personal consequences, not getting on with the job! Then I say out loud. 'F*** it!' I decide to go for it regardless. It frees me from the indecision. Any arguments can be had afterwards.

For the first time in the tour I'm indecisive, I'm struggling. I'm thinking about personal consequences, not getting on with the job! Then I say out loud. 'F* it!' I decide to go for it regardless. It frees me from the indecision. Any arguments can be had afterwards.**

I get hold of a ladder and make my way to the truck. Placing the ladder against the side I shimmy to the top and look down into it. Bolted to the base is the heavy metal framework that supports the large metal firing tubes. I scan each tube. They all seem empty but then … 'Shit' – one tube muzzle is capped. This is not what I had expected to see. Either they would all be empty, or if not the forward part of a bomb would be protruding from the tube. This one is different. Questions fill my mind. Could it be a different type of mortar bomb? Should I get down there and remove the cap? Is there some way I could prevent it from firing? I can't see a firing cable or a switch. Is it about to fire or is it a device that might explode? Too many questions for

The cab has been destroyed by a blast incendiary device. The ladder remains by which I and the CATO scaled the sides.

which there are no answers. I'm already out on a limb. Indecision returns. I withdraw.

Back at the Ops room now everyone is notified of the potential situation. Extra care is to be taken. People are to remain under hard cover unless absolutely necessary. I await the arrival of my team. As time progresses the likelihood of it being a live mortar bomb diminishes.

Then the CATO arrives on the scene. I brief him on the position as it stands. He decides to approach the truck. Climbing down into the truck he pulls off the cap. It's comprised of melted residue from the polythene tarpaulin. The tube's empty. He declares the truck clear. It's safe.

I go on to inspect the remainder of the truck. The damage to the cab has all the hallmarks of a blast incendiary device. If their intention had been to destroy the mortar firing switches, they failed because the crate containing all the switches has been thrown out into the road. I recover all the components intact. I'm amazed at how 'Heath Robinson' the switching arrangements are. It's been assembled in a great hurry, that's obvious. The electric cables are like spaghetti and the car body filler that glues it all together looks as if it's been splashed into place with a paddle. Nonetheless I can't fault them on the fact that the switches did the job they were meant to and all the mortars fired.

The postscript to this incident is that the Royal Engineers work hard throughout the night and repair the outer fencing. Next day there's no sign of the extensive damage to the barracks. The attack doesn't even get a mention in the TV News thus denying PIRA any kudos from all the planning and effort that must have gone into mounting it. I think we score this one as even.

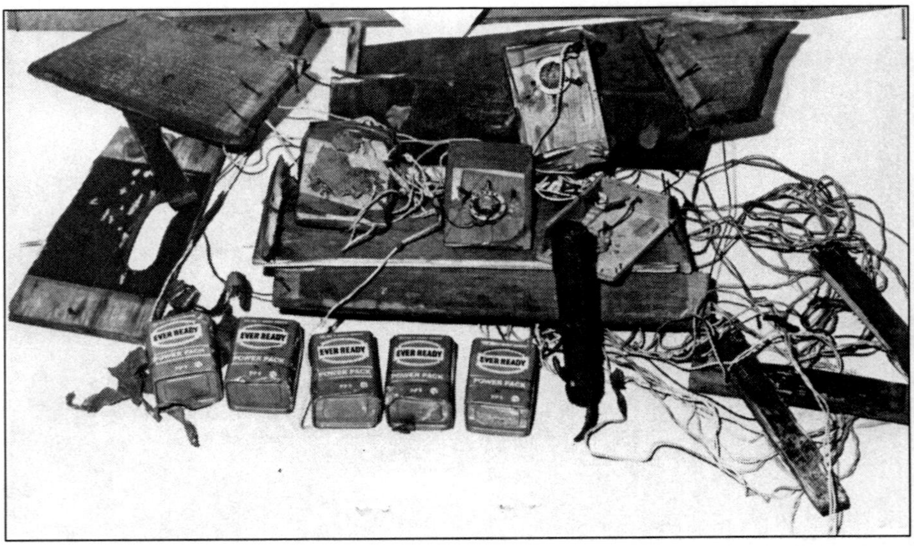

The wood crate containing all the firing switches and batteries was thrown clear of the vehicle by the blast incendiary device.

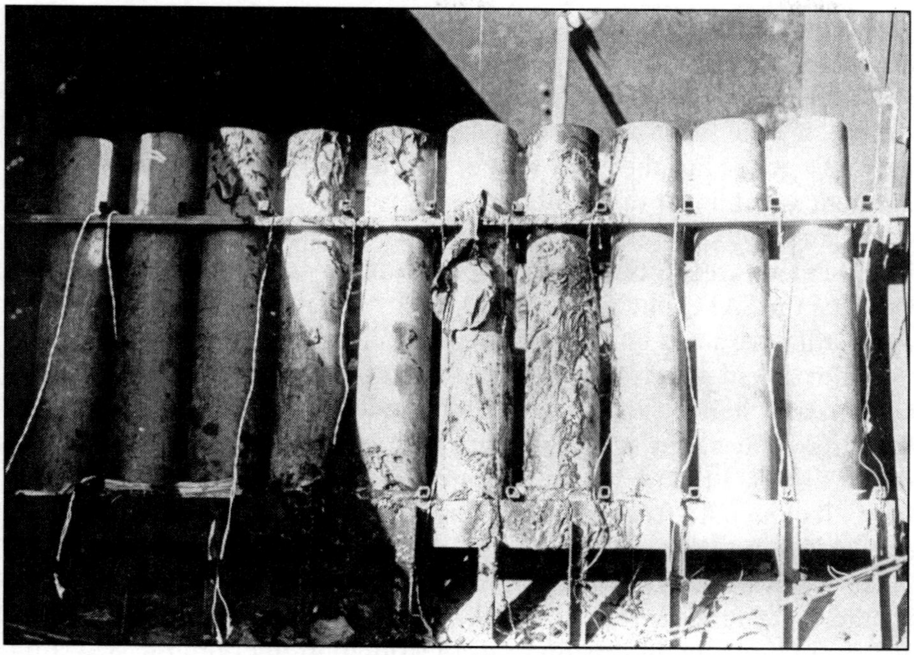

Each tube held an 80lb mortar bomb.

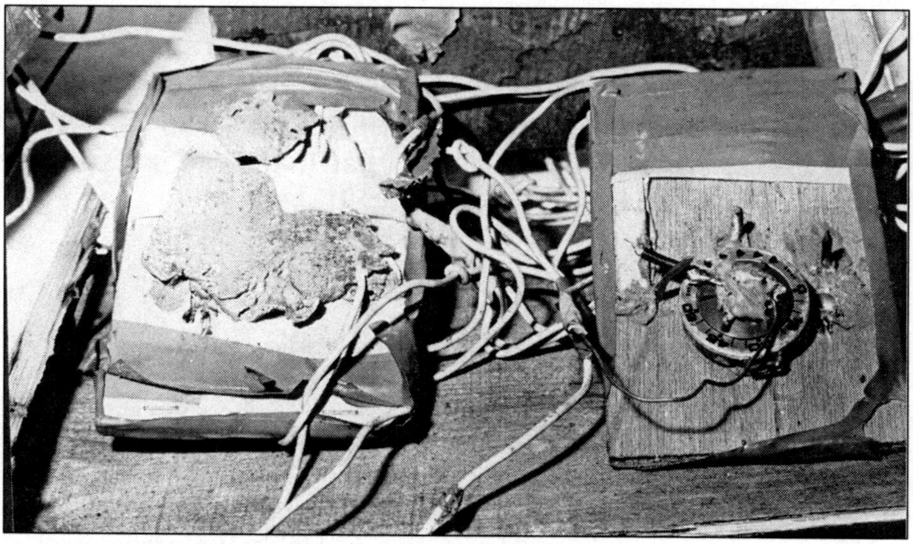

Having been assembled in a real hurry, the switches are pretty rough and ready. If wire cutting is your preferred modus operandi, well there's plenty to choose from here.

I take the opportunity to speak privately with the CATO ref my deteriorating relationship with the SATO. At this point I'm not even sure if the CATO's aware of it. I'm hyped up after weeks of sitting on it and also seriously pissed off that I had had to make decisions today based not on what I thought was right, but on what the SATO's reaction might have been. The CATO knows something is going on and I suspect there are problems elsewhere in the unit. He isn't prepared to discuss the SATO however as that would be bad form. Nonetheless, he goes as far as he can. He's personally very happy with the way things are at the section and he's had good reports from the people I work with. He wants things to continue as they are. Well that's good enough for me. It's the endorsement I need to get mentally back on the case. It may be a cliché but the great weight that lifted off my shoulders at that moment was almost discernible.

Later I get the team together and I pass on the CATO's words. I reassure them we aren't doing anything we shouldn't. I tell them it's a matter between the SATO and I. It's not perfect by any means. It never could be and I still have a bad taste in mouth, but it'll do. Things calm down.

I'm asked to clear a military Storno radio that is found by a civilian and handed in the day after the mortar attack at Newtownhamilton. The radio is a solid state type of technology. I check it out and it's clear. I then have an argument with the 321 Senior Ammunition Technician from Lisburn as to whether I dealt with it appropriately. I know from rumours that he's under pressure to be more exacting and challenging with Operators in respect of their Render Safe Procedures. I have to justify to him every action I took. We get into a silly discussion; unprofessional in my opinion. 321 ain't a particularly happy ship at this time.

He wants things to continue as they are. Well that's good enough for me. It's the endorsement I need to get mentally back on the case. It may be a cliché but the great weight that lifted off my shoulders at that moment was almost discernible.

The new flack jacket

The team is issued with the new flack jackets. These have what I consider relatively small titanium plates fitted front and back. This jacket is designed to stop high-velocity bullets and not just fragmentation, like its predecessor. Unlike its predecessor this jacket is worn underneath the combat jacket. As with anything new there are the critics and it's hard to get ecstatic about anything that's bulky, heavier than its predecessor and limits your movements somewhat. It doesn't look cool either as it gives you a distinct Quasimodo appearance.

In Crossmaglen a foot patrol of the RGJ is fired upon from a school about a hundred yards away. Both lead soldiers are hit dead centre with high-velocity rounds. As one falls he's skimmed by another shot. After the event it's discovered that the titanium plates in both

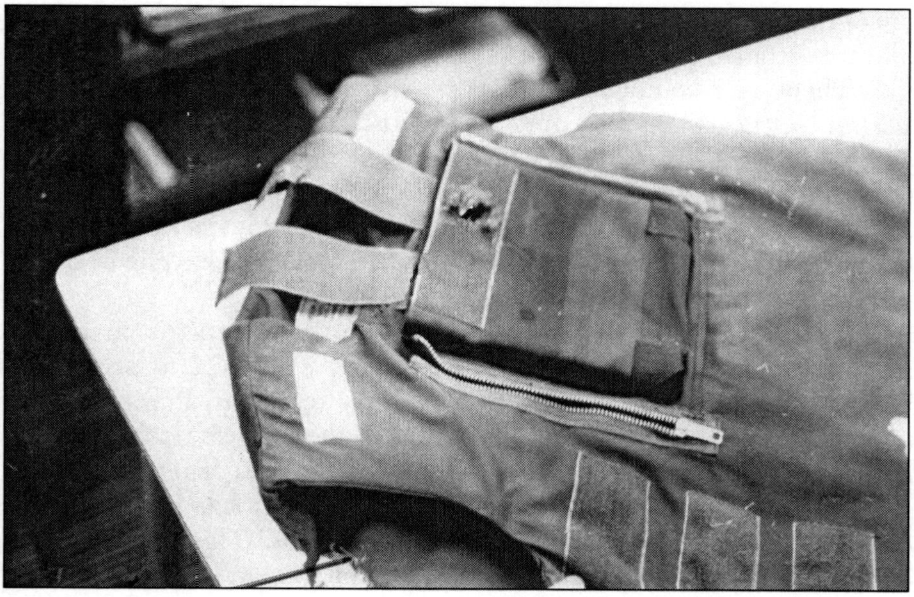

The high-velocity strike mark can be seen on the plate.

jackets have absorbed the impact of the rounds and both soldiers suffer only minor injuries. A miracle?

I now recollect the RPG rocket attack back in February where the Section Commander's life was also saved by this model of jacket. From here on in the new flack jackets have very few detractors; especially me.

A 'force' to be reckoned with

I've struck up a friendship with the RGJ Regimental Sergeant Major, RSM Goddard. Nice bloke. I enjoy his company and the team like him too. He accompanies us on jobs thus providing us with additional protection. People often like to accompany us as they're pretty much guaranteed a bit of excitement! However a different type of excitement arrives at Bessbrook Mill in the shape of an MoD-sponsored Combined Services Entertainment (CSE) show. One act among many is a trio of pretty female dancers who call themselves 'Dee Force'. Eagerly awaited by the troops they do their sexy thing to very loud music and roars of appreciation. Watching them wearing not too much diminishes all thoughts of terrorist bombs and frankly everything else that isn't directly in the line of sight. Their gyrations begin to imbue in me all too familiar physiological feelings. Yes that's right, there are clear and recognisable similarities to how I feel when approaching a device! My pulse rate has increased, adrenalin is flowing, body temperature is rising and my palms sweat. But this time it's actually uncomfortable; even stressful. IEDs are hazardous but beware a trio of bikini-bottomed bombshells in black satin basques!

There is advantage in good networking. After the show, the Warrant Officers' & Sergeants' Mess hosts a dinner to which all the entertainers are invited. The RSM sees to it that I have pride of place seated alongside our very attractive lady guests. They're good fun, chatty and a very welcome relief from the green routine. Later at the bar the girls show us they're still wearing stockings. Excellent! Some distractions up with, they just have to be put!

Towards the end of the dinner the decanter of port is circulated and all glasses charged for the loyal toast. This is a toast to Her Majesty the Queen and a tradition in every regiment. I'm somewhat amazed when the loyal toast is given that all the soldiers remain seated. I turn to a Warrant Officer nearby and query this. 'Isn't that disrespectful to the Queen?' He replies, as he probably has had to do on many occasions, 'Our loyalty was never in doubt.' The idiosyncrasies and traditions of the British Army regimental system – wonderful!

My pulse rate has increased, adrenalin is flowing, body temperature is rising and my palms sweat. But this time it's actually uncomfortable; even stressful. IEDs are hazardous but beware a trio of bikini-bottomed bombshells in black satin basques!

Bikini-bottomed bombshells in black satin basques.

19th May 1981

Group photograph – fatal timing

I deal with two more minor incidents in the interim, a hoax and a false alarm. These keep us on our toes but my mind is beginning to think of other things – handover and home.

Rear – Moggy Wolstenholme, Cyril Simpson, Steve Turner; Front – Davy Marshall, Paul Wharton, Superintendent Caldwell.

I arrange to have a photograph taken of the people I've worked with so closely: the RUC Border Superintendent, the two RUC Liaison Officers, the Royal Engineer Search Adviser and my No. 2 (whose tour is also complete, hence the civvies). The camera clicks, we stand and begin to put the chairs away. Suddenly, '*Baboom!*' The unmistakeable thump of a very large explosion shakes the ground. It reverberates and echoes all around the hills …

The camera clicks, we stand and begin to put the chairs away. Suddenly, '*Baboom!*' The unmistakable thump of a very large explosion shakes the ground. It reverberates and echoes all around the hills …

Explosion, culvert, Chancellors Road, Bessbrook

I make my way quickly to the Ops room. Already the radio traffic is hot. The Ops Officer tells me what he knows. Two Saracen armoured vehicles of Support Company making their way down the Chancellors Road to the Dundalk Road have been attacked. The second vehicle has been hit. It is carrying five soldiers.

I suggest to him that the armoured nature of the vehicle may have protected the soldiers, but from the reports he's receiving the officer is dubious.

The army doctor is quickly on the ground and without any regard to his own safety is reported as running to and fro like a mad man, up and down the area, left and right to try and locate the soldiers in case any are in need of help. This and what he eventually confirms is grim.

I call HQ Lisburn and inform the CATO of what I know. I tell him I need to get to the incident immediately. He says he'll meet me there.

Within 15 minutes I'm in a helicopter over the scene. A massive scar across the whole of the road is unmistakable. The crater must be 50ft across and at least 15ft deep. I thought I would see an armoured vehicle in the vicinity of the crater but of this there is no sign. I need to get on the ground quickly for the incident is already gaining momentum and there are potential dangers from secondary devices.

We approach the RV by vehicle from the south after all the culverts have been searched. The press and TV teams are beginning to arrive. Their apparent lack of compassion for what we are dealing with here is hard for me to stomach and I insist to the police that they

The beginning of the rubble can just be seen at the bend in the lane.

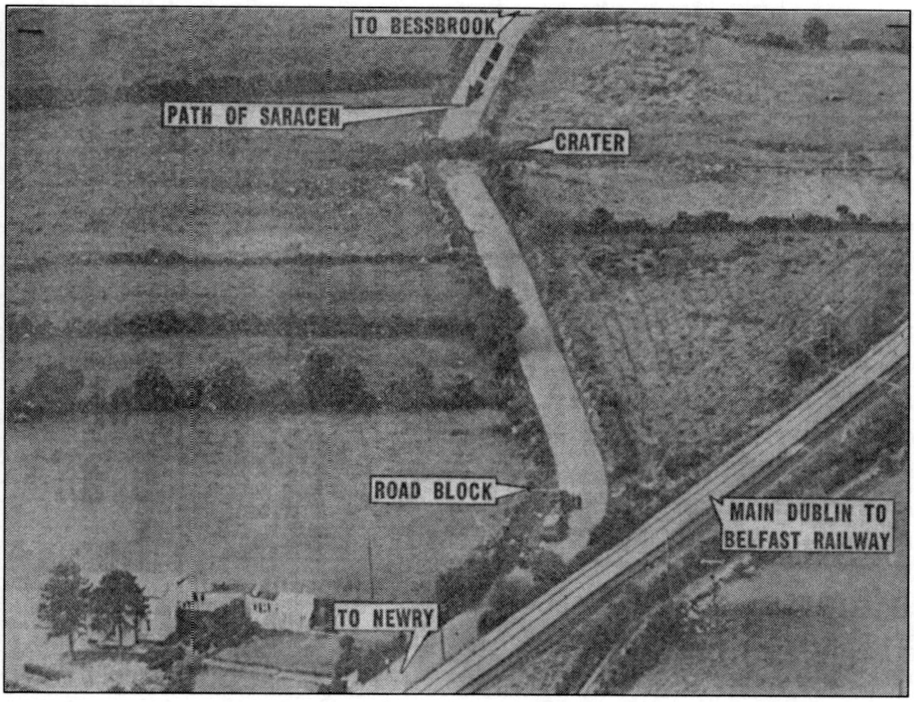

The *Daily Mail* aerial photograph of the scene.

move them way back, well away from the scene. None of us want morbid pictures appearing in the newspapers. We wait by our Transit vehicles as the Royal Engineer Search Teams carry out a 360-degree sweep of the area. Very soon a Command Wire is detected running up the side of the hill towards a housing estate. As I await the go-ahead to enter the scene and clear the crater of any residual explosives a light aeroplane circles above us. Next day I know why when photographs of the scene appear on the front page of all the leading newspapers.

It isn't long before the CATO arrives on the scene and I receive a message to say that he's gone straight to the terrorist firing point which has been located by the Royal Engineers. He asks for some of our equipment to deal with a battery pack which has been found there. I'm about to approach the seat of the explosion so I'm not overly happy about this and I also happen to think he's acting impatiently considering that the last culvert device I dealt with also had a booby trapped battery pack. However, I'm not going to argue with him for obvious reasons. I have some equipment sent to him and he recovers the battery pack and its integral bell push switch, fortunately without any further drama. We recover the terrorist Command Wire which is approximately 500 metres long and buried along its whole length to a depth of about 6 inches. Most of the wire had been in place for at least 6 months. When I eventually get to the terrorist firing point, it is plain to see that the bomber had been sitting in front of a hedge watching the road for quite some time judging by the number of cigarette butts lying around. He let the first vehicle through before pressing the bell push switch. The immediate event would have been the sight of tons of earth and the disintegrating vehicle lifting skywards. This followed within a second by the '*Caboom*' of the pressure wave travelling at probably 3,000 metres a second echoing around the hills. Then everything would have gone into slow motion as the debris reached its zenith and began to fall back to earth. He may have heard the thud as the few remaining vehicle parts of any size struck the ground. As the dust cloud reached 100 feet he would already have turned his back on the scene and be making his way quickly to his getaway car. It was all over in seconds. No fire, no flame, only a massive scar across the landscape pinpointing the tragedy that had just been played out. How many people in the housing estate saw him? I wonder; the only person moving in the opposite direction.

As the dust cloud reached 100 feet he would already have turned his back on the scene and be making his way quickly to his getaway car. It was all over in seconds. No fire, no flame, only a massive scar across the landscape pinpointing the tragedy that had just been played out.

Two years earlier one of our teams was attacked in this way whilst on their way to an incident. Similarly, the second vehicle was taken out and the Royal Signals ECM specialist and his escort were both killed.

The Royal Engineers sweep around the area. But before the dead can be removed we need to be safe and I ensure the immediate area of

CATO and PW take in the size of the pit.

The turret section was thrown 300 metres.

The device had been similar in size to the one we cleared in the same lane three months earlier.

the crater is free from explosives. The explosion had been massive. The device had contained a similar amount of explosives to that used in the Chancellors Road culvert device we dealt with last February. This size is pretty much confirmed when another Bomb Disposal team based at Aughnacloy are tasked to clear an abandoned van. I'm told afterwards that the imprint of six milk churns was apparent on the floor of the van.

Was this PIRA's response to our earlier success? I think it was.

I declare the crater free from explosives and the main recovery begins with the casualties. It's clear that their deaths had been instantaneous. It might seem remarkable, given the damage to the vehicle, but the bodies are recovered almost completely intact. Each of them, held together by their uniform and webbing straps, is carefully lifted into a body bag. It takes a number of people to do this for their skeletal frames are completely shattered.

The armoured vehicle had disintegrated. The turret section is embedded in the ground approximately 300 metres away from the crater. One of the wheels, which must itself weigh a hundred pounds or so has been propelled over a quarter of a mile. It takes the rest of the day and all the following night to recover the many vehicle parts scattered over the fields and also the soldiers' weapons and ammunition.

That evening a service is held at Bessbrook Mill in memory of the

The soldiers' weapons were completely destroyed.

This was the largest section that remained of the armoured vehicle. One wheel was thrown a quarter of a mile.

men who died. The hall is packed with just about everyone not on duty. All want to pay their respects to their fallen comrades. Each person knows it could just have easily been him. Soldiers do reflect society today and few are religious but at times like this the church is indispensable in bringing people together to mourn. The Mill was in a sombre mood for some time afterwards but the security work went on unabated – as it always does. PIRA must know as well as us that an incident like this only serves to increase the army's resolve to defeat the people responsible.

This was the last serious incident I attended. The following week my replacement arrived to take over the Section.

21st May 1981

Handover

I know my replacement well; we've served in the same unit in Germany and attended courses together. As part of the handover we attend an incident together and he leads in the recovery of a number of American bolt action rifles. These weapons have been used to provide a salute at the funeral of a PIRA member. The rifles were spotted by an army covert observation post as they were being spirited away to a hide after the funeral. The recovery from beneath a hedge is straightforward and uneventful.

The remaining handover formalities are carried out to schedule. Weapons, ammunition, explosives and classified documents are checked, accounted for and then signed off. We discuss some of the incidents the team have dealt with. I introduce him to the people he'll be working with.

My time at Bessbrook is ended. The four months have flashed past. The team and I have dealt with 41 incidents in total. Most involved terrorist explosives. Those which had detonators in place are classed as live devices and we had neutralised seven, the largest of which was the Chancellors Road culvert device with its booby trapped firing point. Easily the most complex incident had been the radio controlled attack on the police station at Warrenpoint (which had caused me so much grief with the SATO). The mortar attack at Newtownhamilton was a set piece, well coordinated by PIRA, typical of their modus operandi to kill and gain publicity for it. But by the grace of God and through mainly the efforts of the Royal Engineers, they were thwarted in both. At the second Chancellors Road incident PIRA eventually got the success they were so desperate for, and in a big way. The other devices – the beer keg on the railway line, the blast incendiaries, the ambush devices at the H25 border crossing, the under-car booby traps – were the flotsam and jetsam of an interminable battle of wills that at that time had no end in sight. My tour was a microcosm of the tragedy which is Ulster, written as it is in the shattered lives of the families and friends of those left behind on all sides.

I feel some regret at leaving it all behind. Just at the point, I guess, when I've gained the maximum experience. Having said that, I'm also aware that an Operator can have a shelf life. Without necessarily realising it yourself there are patterns to the way you work which can and will be exploited by the enemy. Four months is enough.

Without necessarily realising it yourself there are patterns to the way you work which can and will be exploited by the enemy. Four months is enough.

The new ATO, Mick O'Neill, is an experienced Warrant Officer and as a second tour Operator knows what he has to do. He will have his own ways of working. Hopefully he will have a better relationship with the SATO than I had.

25th May 1981

Endex

At my final interview with the SATO he presents me with my end-of-tour report. The grading is mediocre but his comments are frankly better than I expected coming from him. His report very much contradicts much of what he said to me immediately following the Warrenpoint job. I'm somewhat wrong-footed by this. In the second section of the report I note that the CATO has endorsed the SATO's comments but has up-rated the grading. He is also kind enough to state that I've been a credit to the Corps.

I'm uncomfortable in the SATO's presence. I don't have much to say to him. Any matters I might have raised go unsaid. To be honest I'm just glad to get out of the place intact and for most of us I think that is enough. I fly out of the Province on Monday 25th May 1981.

Back at Didcot and before proceeding on leave I pay my respects to one of the soldiers killed in the Chancellors Road explosion. I attend his funeral in Abingdon. I never knew the lad, but there is an affinity between all those who serve operationally which is never more apparent than on occasions such as these. I read in the local newspaper that his father is convinced they will be burying a coffin full of rocks; that the lad was blown to bits. I wish I could have assured him that it wasn't the case.

At the end of the ceremony the firing party fires a volley of shots, the Last Post is sounded, the final prayers are said and everyone disperses. The devastated family members are left to try and comfort each other. It's just one event of many. A small measure of the misery that has been brought to thousands of family members and friends since the Troubles commenced. But the cost in these terms is not the key factor and it never will be. Individuals are always sacrificed for principles. Everyone on all sides will keep at it until the politicians can settle it. Whatever the cost, the principles are the overriding factor. It's easy to say and promote, I guess, until you lose someone close.

I'm uncomfortable in the SATO's presence. I don't have much to say to him. Any matters I might have raised go unsaid. To be honest I'm just glad to get out of the place intact and for most of us I think that is enough.

31st May 1981

A further tragedy

Six days after leaving the Province I'm on leave with my wife and children and doing the family rounds. So on the morning of Sunday 31st May we drive from my mother's house in Poulton le Fylde, Lancashire across the Pennines to my wife's parents in Halifax. As I enter their house my father-in-law comments that the BBC are reporting that a soldier has been killed in Newry. I reply that since the army has just pulled out of Newry and the police have taken over patrolling there, I find this surprising. Suddenly, I have a bad feeling and I say as much to my wife.

> **As I enter their house my father-in-law comments that the BBC are reporting that a soldier has been killed in Newry. I reply that since the army has just pulled out of Newry and the police have taken over patrolling there, I find this surprising. Suddenly, I have a bad feeling and I say as much to my wife.**

At 1pm the news comes on the radio again. The soldier killed that morning is named. It's my replacement Mick O'Neill. The shock is jaw dropping. I'm stunned. Anyone who's been thumped in the stomach will know the feeling. I step back and sit down heavily. My wife bursts into tears. I can only imagine what it must be like for his wife and kids; what they're going through.

That afternoon I telephone the Bessbrook Section. The guys are downbeat, in shock. I speak with the No. 2. He tells me the team had been tasked to clear a car abandoned at a road junction near Newry. The car had been re-plated and re sprayed (ie twinned) and then used in the murder of a police officer outside a pub at Whitecross. An anonymous telephone call to the police shortly afterwards reported the car's whereabouts and that they had seen armed men getting out of it.

The team deployed at first light. Given the seriousness of the incident the ATO had gone easy on the car, presumably to preserve any forensic evidence that might be available. Following a series of manual approaches nothing untoward had been discovered. The clearance was nearing completion. Exactly what happened next is unclear. Whilst the No. 2 was in the back of the team Transit getting equipment together, an explosion occurred which blew the car to bits. No one had been watching the car at the time so at first no one knew what had happened. Then it quickly became clear that the ATO was missing. The No. 2 searched for and found the body. He took control of the incident and preserved the scene until the SATO arrived. As the lad had only been in theatre a fortnight himself, I think he did well. The SATO completed the remainder of the investigation. His report reads that in all likelihood it was either a pressure type switch in a seat, or more likely something in the glove compartment. Tests were subsequently carried out on similar cars, but the type of device that killed Mick O'Neill was never confirmed.

The SATO's technical appreciation of the tragedy was professional, but his tendency to lash out surfaced once again. The No. 2 got it in the neck because he wasn't watching the ATO at the time he was killed; even though it was the ATO who had returned to the vehicle without telling anyone. The lad was gutted by the criticism. Suffice to say that there are some officers soldiers are happier to go to the wire with and then there are the others.

I don't know if that IED on the 31st May 1981 had my name on it. I ask myself if I would have tackled it differently and don't like the answer I keep coming up with. We all realised the importance of forensic evidence and I had my own policy of bringing things back in one piece.

Mick O'Neill was in my humble opinion a gallant and brave man. This task was made more dangerous because he was trying to help solve the murder of an off-duty police officer. Unbeknown to him the device had been designed to get him for PIRA knew that in these circumstances he would feel obliged to take risks.

I didn't attend his funeral. By then it had all got to be too much. I couldn't stomach another funeral; any more tragedies. His death came as I was also trying to find time to grieve for the loss of my father. During my tour I had striven to put all thoughts of him completely out of my mind. Looking back I realise too that I was shocked at how close I had come to being killed. Into this mix was the bitterness and anger I felt for the SATO who had so nearly ruined my career. I churned inside with anger. It took years before all that negativity eased its way out of my system and I could at least talk about it without throwing a track. Nonetheless, undoubtedly, I retain some of the scars today.

I don't know if that IED on the 31st May 1981 had my name on it. I ask myself if I would have tackled it differently and don't like the answer I keep coming up with.

Last light

If commanding that unique Unit was a stressful business then in his case, the SATO certainly liked to spread it about. My team and I were unsettled by his aggressive and unreasoning attitude and this impaired my judgement on at least one occasion. In IEDD the strains of the job are enough without that kind of distraction. Those of us who experienced it had a right to expect more.

In IEDD the strains of the job are enough without that kind of distraction. Those of us who experienced it had a right to expect more.

There was something about me that rankled him which I never got to the bottom of. I don't doubt that the SATO was held in high esteem by his superiors and he went on to climb the slippery career pole and in due course achieved the rank of full Colonel. He didn't receive an award for his tour of duty during 1981 but was eventually awarded the OBE for something different. I never met the guy again – why would I want to – except, perhaps, to re-write *his* end-of-tour report.

The CATO will be listed in most soldiers' minds as a 'good bloke', as indeed the vast majority of senior officers are in my experience. He was well respected by those who served under him and I was very glad to have had his support. Perhaps a strength of having two senior appointments preside over 321 EOD Company is that one might be a moderating influence over the other when it became necessary.

The CATO received the OBE for his tour and I expect he went on to greater things. I was glad to meet up with him again when he was the Commanding Officer of the Army School of Ammunition at Kineton in Warwickshire.

The mediocre grade of my end-of-tour report didn't hold me back. A couple of years later I was promoted and soon after selected by the Corps to be a 'Conductor'. This is an ancient and honourable appointment, little publicised, which is conferred on only a few Warrant Officers Class 1 at a time. This small, select band are considered the most senior Warrant Officers in the British Army. This is an assertion that always makes for good arguments at regimental dinners.

Among other things I went on to teach IEDD at the Army School of Ammunition, which didn't in fact change my views of how difficult it was to play the game and get through the Pre-Ops IEDD course. I was commissioned in 1989. In 1995 I retired from the army, having achieved the rank of Major, to become a Programme Manager overseeing portfolios of large business projects.

I very much enjoyed a varied and exciting 28-year career in the army. For a Blackpool lad who left school at 15 with little academic ability and no thought for the future except to serve Queen and Country in one capacity or another, well, it had been quite a ride.

For a Blackpool lad who left school at 15 with little academic ability and no thought for the future except to serve Queen and Country in one capacity or another, well, it had been quite a ride.

Clear down

Our Render Safe Procedures were redeveloped in response to Operator deaths early in the Campaign. They became a catch-all to cover all circumstances but because the techniques weren't viewed as a framework or a tool box, in my opinion they became a bureaucracy. As a bureaucracy they were often overseen in a rigid way. It was almost impossible then to function properly without contravening the rules in one way or another and upsetting the hierarchy. The rules therefore became something to beat you with if someone was of a mind to. Furthermore, despite the rigidity there was a rule for one if not for the others. CATO's and SATO's were pretty much a law unto themselves and worked the RSP's in their own way. I think many of them would accept this.

I maintain that flexibility in the application of RSPs is what was needed and it was getting the balance right that we can argue about. Unfortunately the profession didn't see it like this.

CATO's and SATO's were pretty much a law unto themselves and worked the RSP's in their own way. I think many of them would accept this.

Military leaders, not all, appreciate that plans tend to 'go out the window' on first contact with the enemy. Similarly IEDD situations could and would change from moment to moment and when they did you had to cope with the situation as it evolved around you as best you could. The other agencies involved always had to be considered, whatever the teaching at Pre-Ops courses, and time is always a factor. Yes, your actions may incur additional risk to you, you do your best to reduce them, but these risks go with the job. The people you're supporting need to have confidence in you, know that you have the wherewithal to deal with the situation and that you recognise the pressures they are under too. If they're comfortable with you then you are probably doing OK. When they aren't, and it can happen because IEDD clearance operations can take an awful long time, the Operator needs the backing of the powers that be to support his decisions. Before this problem was recognised, Operators could find themselves under pressure to take action quicker than would otherwise be acceptable today.

An Operator walked a tightrope where discrepancies between what the book says and what he felt was appropriate at any given time could be interpreted as stepping out of line and this in turn could be viewed as recklessness. The upshot of all this is that by expecting Operators to toe the procedural line precisely, any error they make is seen as a contravention. This thinking, I believe, had a bearing on how their deaths were perceived in some quarters.

Recognition

Awards have become an integral part of this work. This subject was the catalyst that prompted the SATO to speak with me at the NI Pre-Operations course. Clearly he had a bee in his bonnet about it. So it was a surprise to me when on 14th December 1981 it was published in the *London Gazette* that I had been Mentioned in Despatches (MID) for gallantry. I am grateful to have been recognised in this way. Among many others I received a congratulatory letter from the CATO and also letters from the Commanding Officers of the two infantry regiments I served with.

I will not dwell on it, for as I say I was very grateful to have been recognised when many others weren't, but the postscript to my MID is that some years afterwards I managed to obtain a copy of the Citation. These are not made available as a matter of course. Reading it I discovered that only the beer keg device and the two Chancellors Road IEDs were mentioned in it. I have always thought that strange.

It's not hard to see why 321 EOD Company became the most decorated unit in the history of the British Army when its men were prepared to walk into the jaws of death and spit in the devil's eye time and time again. In the annals that will undoubtedly be written, it will tend to be those who received the highest honours who are most likely to be remembered first.

So like many things people covet, medals and awards can be a driving influence because, let's face it, there is much kudos in being awarded one. Society uses this as a measure for who they think has been brave and gallant. It is a tenuous measure I'm afraid – or at the very least it only tells part of the story.

Medals and awards

The MID is a Class 4 award. For Class 1–3 gallantry awards, medals are presented and the corresponding letters are allowed to be recorded after the person's name. The MID is instead an oak leaf which is worn on the Campaign Medal. Letters are not recorded after the person's name. In recent years the MID was reviewed and the oak leaf changed from bronze to silver.

It's worth noting in passing that according to governmental machinations in April 2009, a criteria for whether a Gurkha soldier has provided value to our country is if he has received a Class 1, 2 or 3 award.

Some myths about my own profession need exploding here. A study carried out in 1981 by the University of London into fearlessness and courage tried to show that there are physiological differences between Operators who received awards and those who did not. This type of thinking is completely irrational because actually, most guys I know will deal effectively with whatever is put in front of them! What shit does come their way is random because it's down to enemy tactics. Notwithstanding some really heroic acts, whether an ATO is awarded a medal afterwards is subject to a number of variables. For example, it can depend on the weight of IEDD activity at a given point in time. That is, one incident can seem big and important in isolation, but could be seen as routine during high activity. Some people don't get put up for awards for many reasons, some receive lesser awards and some are rejected. The intensity of the Northern Ireland bombing campaign was such that many others could also have won awards if their circumstances had been reported upon differently. Some remarkable acts of courage by ATOs were instead punished – seen as reckless. For example I know of one Staff Sergeant who neutralised two devices placed in derelicts, timed to function as a Protestant march passed by. Because diverting marches can be problematic he walked up and disrupted each device in turn and this allowed the march to pass by uninterrupted. He thought it the right thing to do. But instead of echoing the praise of the troops on the

This type of thinking is completely irrational because actually, most guys I know will deal effectively with whatever is put in front of them! What shit does come their way is random because it's down to enemy tactics.

ground, our people nearly crucified him instead. There will be many other stories like this. The awarding of gallantry medals is hit and miss and some deserving individuals are unfortunately missed.

So my own profession, and also those looking into it, shouldn't get too carried away believing we have a meaningful way of measuring who contributed most. It is not a cast-iron way of quantifying bravery. Group photographs and engraved plaques that reflect award winners in my opinion mainly serve to ignore and undervalue the very many other unsung foot soldiers of this profession who stepped into the dragon's den time and again but didn't receive recognition for it. You might say this type of problem exists everywhere else too. Well OK, but I maintain that it is much more obvious here.

Group photographs and engraved plaques that reflect award winners in my opinion mainly serve to ignore and undervalue the very many other unsung foot soldiers of this profession who stepped into the dragon's den time and again but didn't receive recognition for it.

A system failure?

Did our dead deserve to be recognised? Well, yes, I think many did. The early years of the Irish Campaign were the formative years when most of our losses occurred. It was at a time when the thinking around explosive devices and making them safe still had to be 'cemented'. Our equipment was in its infancy. People felt under pressure to get jobs done quickly. It was also the first time the profession had been pitted against a western terrorist organisation who could call upon first-world technology in the manufacture of their devices. At least one bomb maker during this period came to the party with an electrical engineering background. The tactical options open to the enemy are always many and varied, but Bomb Disposal Operators are not blessed with either hindsight or second sight. Instead, on what is often minimal information they have to make a rapid assessment and then get on with it. In the heat of the moment it is too easy to come to a wrong conclusion. But then it was the Operator alone who entered the dragon's den and if the dragon roared its white-hot breath it was he alone who died. Not someone else. I may be accused of being partisan here, but if that is not an act of gallantry I do not know what is.

In the heat of the moment it is too easy to come to a wrong conclusion.

For much of the early NI Campaign the enemy revised their methods and our techniques had to be redeveloped accordingly. Sometimes we were behind their innovations. Because of this an NI Operator worked not only in a highly hazardous and unpredictable set of circumstances, but it was also a novel experience because everything was so immature and dynamic. I expect too that it was an especially frightening experience, not having the disruptive equipment and remote capability that were developed later. By 1973, 10 Operators had been killed. It was an attrition rate that the profession could not have sustained for any length of time and the development of more effective Render Safe Procedures went on concurrently, consistently and at a pace.

As I have come to appreciate even more from writing this book there were weaknesses in my own questioning technique, misunderstandings and underestimations of the threats. Operators faced each dangerous situation according to an assessment which hinged on speech, hearing and comprehension. In a tense, fast-moving situation what seemed to be the truth of it could easily be flawed. The sheer quantity of incidents that had to be dealt with in the early days, especially in the two cities, Belfast and Londonderry, might also be factored in. Operators could have tasks stacked up and would have to categorise them into an order of priority. In one four-month tour an Operator could be called upon to deal with well over 100 incidents. On each of those separate occasions this ordinary guy, with a nominal amount of training, entered a dragon's den voluntarily on behalf of Queen and Country and at that point his family and friends were left behind – not once but every time.

Operators faced each dangerous situation according to an assessment which hinged on speech, hearing and comprehension. In a tense, fast-moving situation what seemed to be the truth of it could easily be flawed.

When we were transitioning from the passive to the offensive strategies Operators were expected to sandbag a device in order to reduce the likelihood of collateral damage since the thinking was that the brick walls of a shop were worth endangering these men's lives for. For those who died, who felt the full force of the dragon's breath, it was the very act of walking into the dragon's den that was in my opinion the gallant act.

In the Northern Ireland conflict the medals awarded for this work were pretty much based on hypotheticals. For example, the device might have gone off, or it might have caused X amount of damage. Citations were written up on how long a clearance took or how many manual approaches were necessary. Fair enough, but hey, many devices for which people received top awards would probably never have gone off at all; some of mine too. Of course this is after the fact and I don't want to decry many whose awards were well deserved. But there can be no argument as to which devices were the most dangerous; they were those that killed our colleagues. There can be no question as to who sacrificed more; it was their wives and their families. There can be no question as to who was let down; it was them.

For those who died, who felt the full force of the dragon's breath, it was the very act of walking into the dragon's den that was in my opinion the gallant act.

How should we measure the work? Well I think the value is in having people who are prepared to get qualified, who are willing to take the risk and who will step into the dragon's den on behalf of society. I think that this itself is worthy of some form of recognition. I mean, it's not the money is it? No one was paid anything extra for doing this job.

Why weren't our people recognised? Well this appears to have been a policy matter. Up until 1982 (the Falklands) the MoD apparently did not allow Gallantry medals to be awarded posthumously except for the VC, GC or Mentioned in Despatches. These are class 1 and class 4 awards; no class 2 or 3 awards. This was contrary to the policy of other services like for example the police force. I have to confess that I came by this information very late in the writing of this book. In one way it is a relief to find that it was MoD bureaucracy and not my profession that had fallen down on the job. Pity there was no Joanna Lumley to fight the case back then.

A consequence of this 'policy' is that many of us thought that those killed had been found by our own hierarchy to be partly culpable for their own deaths, that the lack of an award was to encourage adherence to procedures. This thinking was occasionally visible in our training. Many of us regret that now.

Whilst I have argued that oversight of the Render Safe Procedures could sometimes be too rigid, it was important to have them and for this we have those who didn't return from the long walk to thank. New techniques were introduced or modified as a direct result of the lessons learned from those tragedies. It was those guys who were the pathfinders in this business and in my opinion the real heroes; every single one of them. No one on our side is to blame for the deaths of our Operators; least of all themselves. It was the war.

Some people had a strange view that Operators came to the job with something like a death wish; a willingness to risk all for the glory. I don't think so. I think most people just wanted to do a good job and get home. Doing a 'good job' would in my opinion be measured in terms of meeting the needs and expectations of the populace and other agencies involved. That's the reality, and in the real world it requires additional risks to be taken. These are personal risks taken with the best of intentions. A man should not be crucified for that.

When forgetting can be harder than remembering

By mid-1988 I had become a Warrant Officer Class 1 and the Senior Ammunition Technician at the Army School of Ammunition at Kineton in Warwickshire. Time and time again I'd watch VIP visitors discussing the varnished boards which listed all our award winners, until finally I'd had enough. I wrote to the Ammunition Technician fraternity across the globe asking if they would support the need for a memorial to our dead. In June of that year I consolidated the 100% positive responses into a letter which I staffed to the Commanding Officer of the Army School of Ammunition, Lt Col Des Townsend. He was sympathetic. His second-in-command Major Terry Cosgrove took the idea to the school graphics artist Ray Gilder who designed a memorial garden incorporating a statue of an Operator. The Corps and the Ammunition Technician profession ran with the idea and through the efforts of many who raised the funds and because of those who kindly provided them, the EOD Memorial at Kineton in Warwickshire, true to Ray's drawing, was finally dedicated two years later on 21st June 1991 at a service conducted by the Chaplain General. Displayed is a name plaque for each Operator killed since 1945. Behind each one of those plaques is another story that one day might get told. It's a story of ordinary people, who with a minimum

Behind each one of those plaques is another story that one day might get told. It's a story of ordinary people, who with a minimum amount of training, entered a real dragon's den, left behind their family and friends and laid down their lives for their country.

amount of training, entered a real dragon's den, left behind their family and friends and laid down their lives for their country. This memorial is for all time and for all to see, a tangible means by which this sacrifice can be recognised, respected and remembered.

Unfortunately, on the day of the memorial's dedication only those who had been awarded medals were invited to appear in the group photograph. Insensitive? I think so given that the families and other

A testimony to ordinary but gallant men who entered a real dragon's den and gave their all for their country.

veterans were present. The controversy between those who were lucky enough to be honoured by the system and our dead was not understood even then, and perhaps for many it still isn't. Going forward, will history record the glory of those honoured, or honour sufficiently our glorious dead?

The Northern Ireland Campaign is over now. As I write, our people are carrying out this same work in other campaigns across the world and have been for some years. The equipment will be better but the bombs are bigger and I expect the scenarios are even more complicated. Even so it will always be the Northern Ireland Campaign that defined the IEDD profession, brought it to maturity and made it fit to fight the 'asymmetrical' type wars of the twenty-first century. On that journey 17 gallant Operators serving with 321 EOD Company died, whose deaths went unrecognised by the honours and awards system. It was an aberration because everyone on our side, at the very least, has a lot to thank them for.

Lightning Source UK Ltd.
Milton Keynes UK
31 August 2010

159207UK00006B/48/P